Parent-Child Attachment Play

Using Reflective Functioning to empower parents and carers as change agents in their own families

Debi Maskell-Graham

big toes little toes

big toes little toes
Registered with the Charity Commission for England and Wales

Registration No. 1152716

For information contact:

http://www.bigtoeslittletoes.org

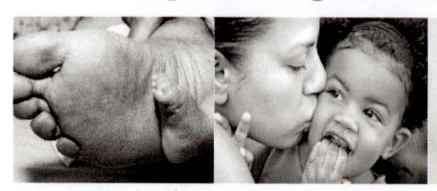

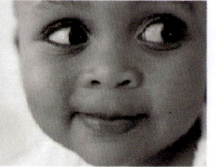

Parent-Child Attachment Play:
Using Reflective Functioning to empower parents and carers as change agents in their own families

Copyright © 2017 Debi Maskell-Graham

All rights reserved. No part of this book may be reprinted or reproduced or used in any form or by electronic, mechanical, or other means, now known or hereafter invented, including photocopying and recording, or in any information storage or retrieval system, without express permission from the publisher.

Images: iStock and Debi Maskell-Graham

Cover Design: Sophie Maskell

First published 2017
ISBN: 978-0-9957628-2-4

Printed by Biddles Books, King's Lynn, Norfolk

For parents and carers everywhere.

About the Author

Debi Maskell-Graham is Director of big toes little toes, a charity registered in England and Wales. Over the last 30 years, she has been developing and facilitating innovative and strengths-based practice from within and alongside communities in the UK, and now around the globe. As a play therapist, researcher, trainer and consultant, she is passionate about translating attachment theory and the latest peer-reviewed research into playful, accessible and effective programmes to strengthen the parent-child relationship. Debi is author of many papers, professional briefings and another book for practitioners "Reflective Functioning and Play: Strengthening attachment relationships in families from pregnancy to adolescence" published in 2016. She is known for her playfulness, humour and very human approach to work with families and children.

Notes to the Reader

To aid the flow of the text, practitioners, parents, carers and children are referred to in the feminine.

Parents and carers are referred to equally as this work is very much for all those who raise children.

Parent-Child Attachment Play resources for practitioners can be found at: www.bigtoeslittletoes.org

Acknowledgements

Whilst writing a book can seem a lonely proposition, it is actually very much a team effort. I would like to thank a number of wonderful folks who have either inspired this book or helped in its creation.

My first thanks go to the many parents and carers who I have had the great privilege of getting to know. Thank you for growing to trust me and for trying the developing elements of the Parent-Child Attachment Play method. Listening to parents and carers over the years has made me realise just how hard being a parent can sometimes be. My own experience as a single mum raising two beautiful and feisty girls also provided rich experiences and insight into the challenges of raising 21st-century children and teenagers.

I would also like to thank Tara Mcdonald (currently living and working in Thailand) for her amazing belief in this work and her help in expanding it to far-flung places. You are fabulous! Thank you to Caroline Sullivan in South Africa, who has worked with me in Kenya and continues to work in Cape Town, using and testing the skills in this book with very vulnerable parents and carers. More thanks go to Ruth McDonagh, Linsey McNelis, and Sophia Giblin for championing the PCAP approach and trying so hard to cherish the spirit in which it has been created.

My heartfelt thanks go to Risë vanFleet, who is one of the best people on the planet! Your filial therapy work with families is what got me started thinking about how to combine my research into Reflective Functioning with an effective method to see parents and carers blossom as change agents in their own families.

Finally, I would like to thank my own amazing family, who believe in me and the work of big toes little toes with such passion and love. Sophie, thank you for coming to India and Kenya with me to help our work adapt and mould in some of the most vibrant places in the world. Chloe, thank you for coming to South Africa and supporting me in the training of large numbers of social workers, psychologists, NGO workers and others. Thank you, too, for the

Acknowledgements

best vegan chocolate cupcakes in the world! Peter, my husband and best friend, thank you so much for the quiet and uninterrupted time I needed to write this book. You are the unsung hero of my work.

Debi Maskell-Graham, December 2016

Contents

About the Author iv
Notes to the Reader v
Acknowledgements vi
Introduction 1

Part 1: An overview of Parent-Child Attachment Play 9
    What is Parent-Child Attachment Play? 9
    What is the theory and evidence base for Parent-Child Attachment Play? 13
    What are the ten steps of Parent-Child Attachment Play? 19
    What are the three skills that parents and carers develop in Parent-Child Attachment Play? 20
    Skill 1: Play 21
    Skill 2: Containment 28
    Skill 3: Head, Heart and Hands (Reflective Functioning) 35
    Where does the skill-sharing method for Parent-Child Attachment Play originate? 41
    Which parents/carers is Parent-Child Attachment Play for? 42
    How do I know that Parent-Child Attachment Play works? 43
    Can Parent-Child Attachment Play be used in different formats? 43
    How long does the Parent-Child Attachment Play method take? 44
    How much does Parent-Child Attachment Play cost to deliver? 45
    Can Parent-Child Attachment Play be delivered privately? 46
    Who can deliver Parent-Child Attachment Play? 46
    What skills do Parent-Child Attachment Play practitioners need? 47

Parent-Child Attachment Play

What training and support do Parent-Child Attachment Play practitioners need? 48
What ethical framework do Parent-Child Attachment Play practitioners adopt? 49
What evaluation tools can I use to measure the outcomes of Parent-Child Attachment Play? 50
What resources do I need to deliver Parent-Child Attachment Play? 51
How do I become a licensed Parent-Child Attachment Play practitioner? 53

Part 2: The 10-step method 55

Step 1: Building a relationship with parents and carers 55
Step 2: Assessing need, setting goals and optional parent-child play observation 61
Step 3: Play (Skill 1) 63
Step 4: Containment (Skill 2) 67
Step 5: Plan home-based playtimes and review skills 1 and 2 ... 70
Step 6: Head, Heart and Hands (Reflective Functioning) (Skill 3) 71
Step 7: Begin playtimes at home 76
Step 8: Transfer skills to problematic areas of home life 78
Step 9: Gently move to phone/text/ email support 79
Step 10: Ending and reporting 80

Part 3: The one-step or "light" version 83

Conclusion 87

Appendix 1 What is PCAP? 89

Appendix 2 10-step method Practitioner Summary 93

Appendix 3 Our PCAP Programme Planner 97

Appendix 4a Practitioner guidance for Play skill 101

Appendix 4b Parent/carer handout for Play skill 105

Appendix 5a Practitioner guidance for Containment skill 109

Appendix 5b Parent/carer handout for Containment skill 113

Appendix 6a Practitioner guidance for Head, Heart and Hands (RF) skill 117

Appendix 6b Parent/carer handout for Head, Heart and Hands (RF) skill 121

Appendix 7 Extra activities to support development of the three skills 125
    Skill 1: Play (and mini-kit) 126
    Skill 2: Containment 126
    Skill 3: Head, Heart and Hands (RF) 127

Appendix 8 Karen's story annotated for evidence of parental Reflective Functioning capacity 129

Appendix 9 Frequently asked questions 133

References 137

Postscript from the author 143

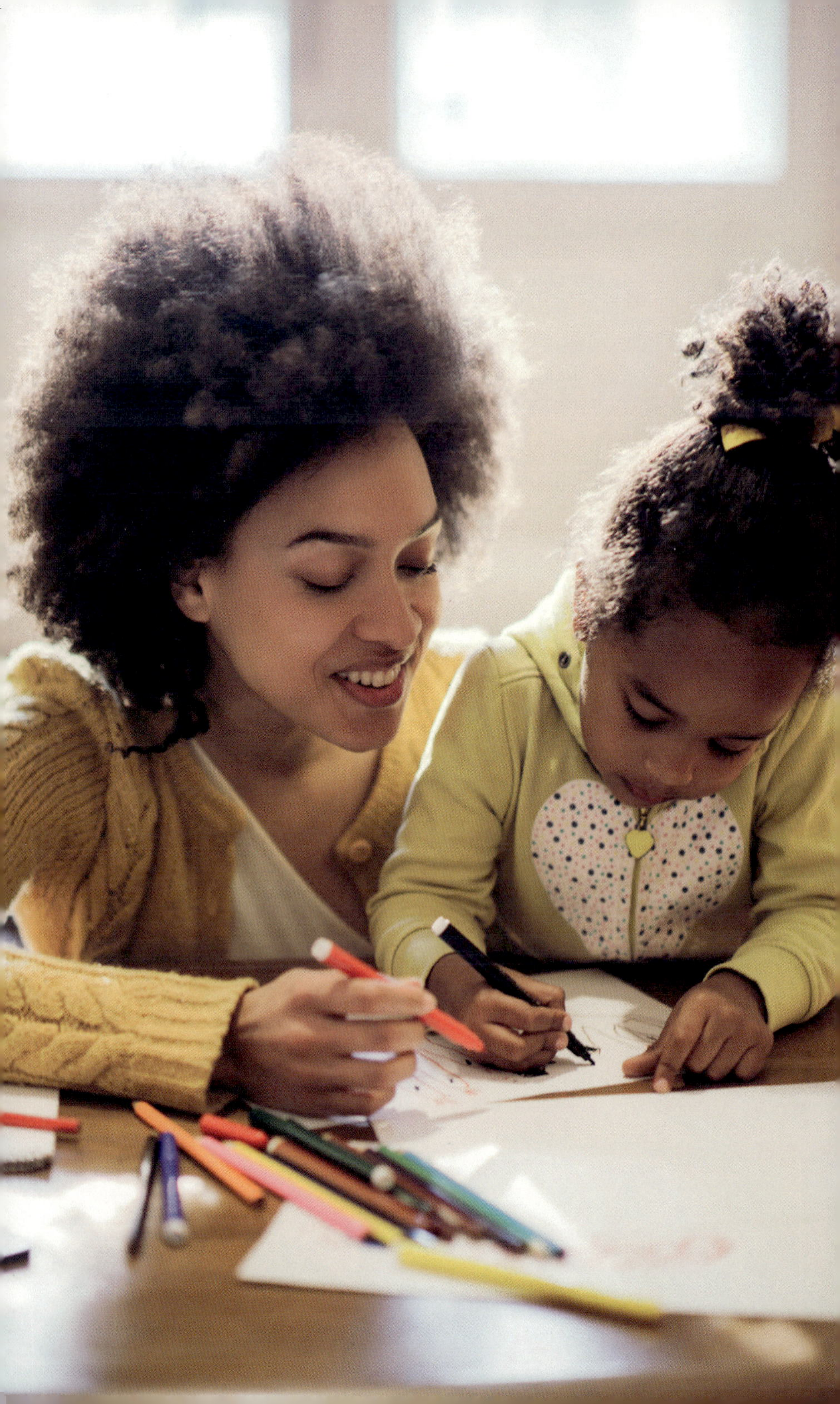

Introduction

There can be no keener revelation of a society's soul than the way in which it treats its children.

Nelson Mandela, 1995

Parents and carers have a challenging job to do in raising happy and successful children in today's society. They have no real training and are faced with an array of advice which is often contradictory. Added to this, they are frequently blamed for their children's behaviour and even get lumped together as a group to be shamed for the state of society today. Some parents/carers have chosen to adopt and foster children whose personal history is complex and results in a legacy of relationship difficulties going forward. Society seems to have limited kindness and tolerance when parents/carers are seen to struggle with their children's behaviour, particularly in public.

Over recent years I have been looking at the many approaches and interventions to support parents/carers with child-rearing. I have been struck by the use of words such as "at-risk", "troubled", "hard-to-reach" and "disengaged" to describe target parents and carers. Of course, these words reflect the reality of some families and the well-documented risks to the children who live within them. However, we are in danger of pathologising parenting and alienating the very families who may benefit from the right kind of help. Reducing the social stigma and negative labelling around families may encourage and motivate engagement in many more who would like to enjoy improved relationships with their children and teenagers. Whilst social and economic deprivation are known risk factors to the quality of parent-child relationships, *most* families struggle with their children and teenagers at some point. Families do not always conform to the stereotypes of those who are seen to need help. A needs-led rather than problem-focused approach might be a better and more productive way to think about how best to offer non-judgemental services that families feel encouraged to access. I would very much like to live in an empathic society where support and help for families is normalised and celebrated.

In addition, there is a fundamental problem around the narrative of "parenting". I have come to call this the "parenting paradox". By constructing interventions around the parenting concept, support services are perhaps in danger of adopting a deficit model. The narrative around this model could act as a barrier for parents and carers who are well aware that they need support with their children and family life. Even by offering "parenting programmes" to families, the narrative risks being "you are not yet an adequate parent" and, even more disempowering, "we will teach you how to be a good parent". Even with the best intentions, the offer of parenting programmes to parents and carers can activate inadequacy and even shame. How can we change this narrative? How can we approach raising children from a strengths-based philosophy, one which empowers parents as the growing experts in their child's care? One which normalises support for families raising children in a complex 21st-century world?

"Parenting" and "parenting styles" are relatively new concepts and refer to the set of principles and behaviours adopted by parents and carers to raise their child(ren). For me – and a significant body of researchers and practitioners alike – they are also problematic.

Not least, developmental psychologists are still exploring the links between parenting styles and their effect on child development and outcomes over time. It is still not proven if this is a true cause and effect impact. It is likely that other factors, such as parent and child temperaments, cultural factors and levels of child resilience, also play their part.

A key researcher in the development of parenting styles is Diana Baumrind, whose studies revealed four key dimensions of parenting: discipline strategies, warmth and nurturance, communication styles, and expectations of child maturity and self-control (Baumrind, 1967).

From these domains, Baumrind went on to propose three main parenting styles: authoritarian (high control/low warmth), authoritative (high control/high warmth) and permissive (low control/high warmth). Researchers later proposed a fourth style: uninvolved (low control/low warmth) (Maccoby and Martin, 1983).

Authoritarian parenting requires children to follow the strict rules established by the parents or carers. Failure to comply results in punishment. Another key characteristic is that parents do not explain the rules or the reasons behind them. Parents are demanding but generally unresponsive to their children. Baumrind describes these parents as obedience- and status-oriented.

Authoritative parenting describes a style in which rules and guidelines are established, but in a more democratic manner. Parents are responsive to their children and take their views into account. When rules are broken, these parents tend to be less punitive than their authoritarian counterparts. They tend to have high expectations of their children but temper this with support and nurturance.

Permissive parenting describes parents who have few demands to make of their children. Discipline is rarely used and these parents are mainly responsive and engaged. Permissive parents may expect considerable self-regulation in their children and avoid situations of confrontation. They are generally nurturing and communicative.

Uninvolved parenting is characterised by few demands, low responsiveness, and little empathy and communication. The child's basic needs may be met but these parents are generally detached from and/or disinterested in the child. In extreme cases, parents may be rejecting or even neglectful of the child's needs.

Authoritarian parenting styles are generally associated with children who are obedient and proficient, but with compromised happiness, social competence and self-esteem. Authoritative parenting styles tend to result in children who are happy, capable and successful across all domains. Permissive parenting often results in children who score poorly in self-regulation and happiness. Interestingly, these children are more likely to experience problems with authority and may underperform at school. Unsurprisingly, uninvolved parenting generates the poorest outcomes for children. These children tend to lack self-control, have low self-esteem and are less competent than their peers (O'Connor and Scott, 2007).

At first glance, it seems that an authoritative parenting style is most desirable and generates the best outcomes for children. However, it is more complicated than this. Much of the research, which is North American in origin, shows good outcomes for authoritative parenting across European-American population groups but not so for African-American and Asian-American populations. Also, in research terms, the correlations between parenting styles and child outcomes are not strong. Other factors must be in play, including culture, children's individual temperaments, and social factors and influences. There may also be important omitted variables; for example, certain families may be more likely to provide extra-curricular activities for their child(ren) or encourage reading from a young age. Both of these factors are likely to influence the outcomes for children.

Lastly, it is difficult to tease out the actual effects of parenting behaviour because there is likely to be a reverse causality at work. For example, a child may be difficult, so the parent gets frustrated and angry with her. However, it could also be that the parent, in becoming frustrated and angry, results in a child with difficult behaviour. Proving just a one-way effect is problematic.

Baumrind's own work identified a small group of parents who did not fit into her parenting styles paradigm. These parents appeared to enjoy successful and happy relationships with their children yet exhibited none of the key characteristics of authoritarian, authoritative or permissive parents (Greenspan, 2006). This group is of great interest because they confound the parenting styles model.

So far, we have seen that "parenting" is a tricky concept both in social and research terms. Certainly, the empirical evidence on parenting styles is perhaps limited in its ability to show the relative importance of parental behaviour or parenting styles.

This book approaches the whole concept of being a parent or carer from a completely different viewpoint. Rather than seeing parent-child relationships in terms of more or less helpful parenting behaviours or styles, we are going to focus on the *nature* and *quality* of the dynamic dyadic parent-child relationship. Fortunately, the research community has much to say on this.

Consequently, this book presents an innovative and strengths-based method to strengthen the parent-child relationship by empowering parents and carers as change agents in their own families. Parent-Child Attachment Play (hereafter generally referred to as PCAP) is a relatively simple and effective method utilising three key elements: a home-based play session between parent or carer and child, a few rules (choices) to contain the play and a known attachment-generative mechanism.

The PCAP method aims to strengthen the parent-child relationship as the context in which both child and parent behaviours and interactions take place. Strengthen the nature and quality of the

Introduction

relationship and, in turn, the habitual and engrained negative behaviours begin to lose their potency. Focus on parents and carers "being" with their children rather than "doing" things with or to them, and help unhelpful behaviours or patterns diminish.

In addition, PCAP recognises that parental capacity to enjoy improved interaction with children is reduced by overwhelming stress. This stress can be internal – for example, difficult mind and emotional states such as losing your temper or weeping with frustration, which seem to take over; or external – for instance, everyday worries such as housing problems, wider family problems, paying the rent on time, work pressures and childcare difficulties. PCAP is designed to facilitate both relational quality and internal/external stress reduction.

The book is in three parts.

Part 1, "An overview of Parent-Child Attachment Play", introduces the method to readers and outlines its principles, three skills and 10-step method in brief. It also outlines the theory and empirical research underpinning the method. The multiple formats for delivery are discussed, along with the ethical framework in which PCAP is embedded. Practitioner skills and training are addressed, with emphasis on the need for reflective practice and mentoring support. This section concludes with practical matters such as practitioner licensing, evaluation measures, resourcing and ongoing support through various online provision.

Part 2, "The 10-step PCAP method", moves on to present the process in fine detail. This is animated by creative examples and the presentation of a case study which journeys through the ten steps with readers.

Part 3, "PCAP as a one-step or 'light' approach", shares how the very essence of PCAP can be shared with parents and carers in one or just a few meetings. Perhaps the practitioner only has one opportunity to offer a practical attachment idea to a family. Perhaps the practitioner is confident that the parent or carer in front of her actually only needs a simple idea to try. Maybe the practitioner is meeting the parent to review services which are already underway for her child, for example a psychological or developmental therapy. The practitioner can see that a simple PCAP idea could support the ongoing work with the child.

Ironically, the other helpful time to use a one-step or light approach is when things are extremely difficult between parent/carer and child, to the point where it is unlikely that the child will be interested in sharing play or activity time at home with the parent/carer. In these cases, a single idea can be shared for the parent or carer to attempt to build a bridge back to a more stable parent-child relationship. Of course, in this example, additional intervention will likely be needed to support this relationship and avoid a damaging breakdown.

The Appendices at the back of the book are packed with resources needed by the budding PCAP practitioner, including handouts for parents and carers, planning and skill guidance sheets for practitioners, and additional activities which practitioners might use for the creative and playful development of the three PCAP skills. They also include a list of frequently asked questions that may be helpful as practitioners begin to adopt this method.

Online resources and materials can also be found at www.bigtoeslittletoes.org. "big toes little toes" is a charitable incorporated organisation registered with the Charity Commission for England and Wales. It exists to support practitioners around the globe with high-quality resources, research and training for those specialising in the attachment and play approach.

As we move on to introduce PCAP and its various elements, we begin to address those all-important questions for practitioners:

- What is Parent-Child Attachment Play?
- Why and how does it work?
- Who does it work for, and in what circumstances and contexts?
- How do I deliver it?

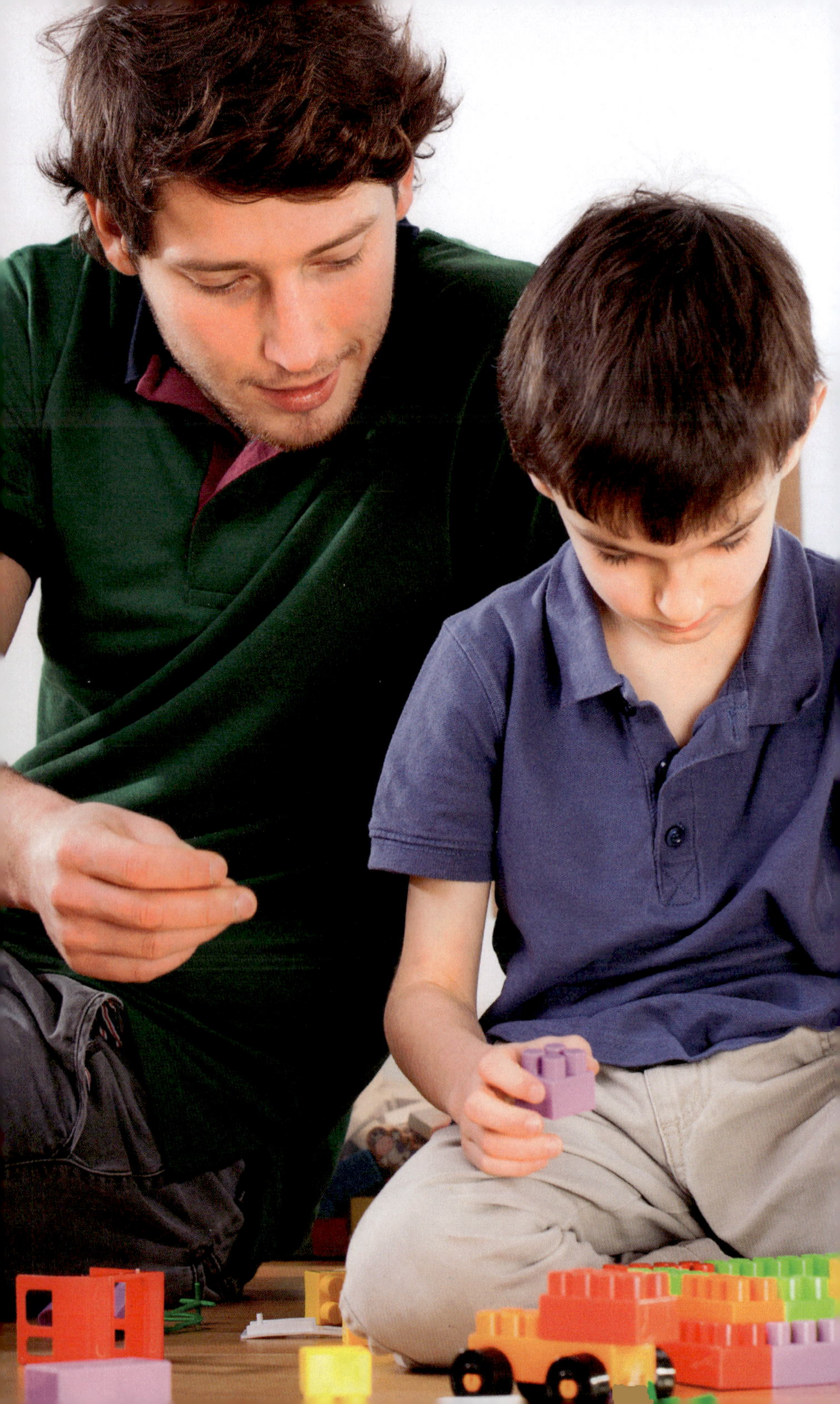

Part 1:
An overview of Parent-Child Attachment Play

What is Parent-Child Attachment Play?

PCAP is an innovative and playful ten-step method to empower parents and carers as the change agents in their own families. Fundamentally, it enables parents and carers to strengthen the quality of relationship they share and enjoy with their child(ren), both inside and outside the family home. It involves the PCAP practitioner working with the parent/carer and not directly with the child (although there are a few occasions when the practitioner might be present to support the dyad). The relationship between the practitioner and parent/carer establishes the context in which the parent-child relationship can blossom. PCAP practitioners can gently interrupt the known problem of attachment transmission evident in many families, in which relational difficulties appear to pass down the generations.

PCAP involves sharing three skills with parents and carers: play (and the creation of a shoebox or bag of toys/activities designed around the preferences of the child); containment (managing time, environment, emotions and child choices); and an attachment-generative mechanism known as Reflective Functioning. Once parents and carers feel confident in the skills, they begin a short weekly "You and Me" playtime at home with their child. This creates a "ring-fenced" opportunity to practise the skills and enjoy a new way of being with the child. Once the skills are well-established, the parent/carer is helped to transfer them to problematic areas of home life. Throughout the process, the parent/carer is supported by a PCAP practitioner.

Security of parent-child attachment in childhood is well-known to predict children's outcomes across the lifespan in all domains including social, economic, psychological and educational (see, for example, Greenberg, 1999; Green and Goldwyn, 2002; WHO, 2004). It is also linked with school-readiness and social competence on entry to education (Rispoli et al., 2013). Attachment security in early childhood can even predict cognitive ability in 20-year-olds (Moutsiana et al., 2014). Attachment theory and its operational mechanisms are explored in depth later in this Part.

In turn, PCAP rests on the secure and trusting relationship which grows between the parent/carer and the PCAP practitioner. This relationship sets the scene for the nurturance of the three key and transformative skills or mechanisms. These skills are guided by and nurtured through a straightforward ten-step PCAP process. Figure 1.1 below illustrates how these elements fit together.

PCAP is a theory-driven and evidence-based method whose content mobilises attachment theory and the very latest empirical evidence on how attachment is mechanised within the parent-child relationship. Its skill-sharing method has been inspired by the methodology of Filial Therapy and the work of Bernard and Louise Guerney, Risë vanFleet and Virginia Ryan (Guerney and Ryan, 2013; vanFleet, 2014). Filial Therapy is a specialised play therapy technique in which parents and carers are taught how to support their children using basic play therapy skills. Its method has provided an outline model of skill transference for PCAP. However, PCAP is not itself a play therapy technique. Whilst play is used as a developmentally-appropriate activity for parents and carers to share with their children, PCAP focuses on a single attachment-generative mechanism and internal/external stress reduction in the parent/carer. PCAP's theory, evidence base and model are discussed in detail later.

Whilst PCAP's theoretical and empirical roots are comprehensive, PCAP itself is a straightforward and "stripped-back" method designed for ease of use by a range of practitioners and professionals.

An overview of Parent-Child Attachment Play

PRINCIPLES	SKILLS	METHOD
Guiding parent/carer and PCAP practitioner relationship	Three skills to empower parent/carer as change agent in their own family	10-step method to share, practise and embed the three skills into family life
A strengths-based approach	**1. Play**	1. Referral and building practitioner-parent relationship
Parent/carer as expert in their own child and family situation	Weekly parent/carer-child playtime using mini-kit of toys and/or activities - play designed around child's needs and preferences	2. Assessment of need
Empowering parents and carers as change agents in their own family		3. Play skill and mini-kit prepared
		4. Containment skill
	2. Containment	5. Plan parent-child home playtimes and review
An "inside-out" process based on internal motivation and relationship quality, not behaviour modification	Agreed non-punitive rules around playtime, play space, use of toys and child choices	6. Head, Heart and Hands (Reflective Functioning) skill
Reflective Functioning as mechanism to bridge any relational gaps in parental history	**3. Head, Heart, Hands (Reflective Functioning)**	7. "You and Me" playtime begins at home
		8. Roll out playtime skills to everyday family life
Learning through playfulness, curiosity and supported practice	Attachment-generative mechanism for parents and carers to practise during home playtimes	9. Change to phone/text/email support
		10. Ending

Figure 1.1: What is Parent-Child Attachment Play?

The design of the model is to make its tools widely available to families and suitably-skilled practitioners across culture, context and need. However, "simple" does not mean "easy", and PCAP practitioners are highly skilled in relationship-building with families and in the operational mechanisms of the method.

Wherever possible, parents and carers need to be supported to become the change agents within their own families. Equipping families from within offers a respectful and sustainable approach to strengthening security of attachment in the parent-child relationship. It offers an "inside-out" method in which parents and carers can build on their role as the expert in recognising and meeting their child's needs. It avoids long-term dependency on professional services and the inherent danger in "doing things to" families rather than enabling internal resources and strengths to grow from within.

Essentially, PCAP works by meeting the relational needs of parents and carers first. This is achieved via the relationship between the parent/carer and the PCAP practitioner. Some parents and carers may not have had a positive experience of childhood themselves, and even those who have often have alternative ideas about how they would like to raise their own children. Regardless of family history and experiences, most parents and carers have a desire for positive outcomes for their children. However, the reality of day-to-day life can make it difficult for parents and carers to overcome negative patterns in family interactions. This is true for all families and not just those considered to be at risk through social or economic deprivation or other known factors. PCAP is designed to:

- provide authentic relational support to come alongside parents and carers
- acknowledge and validate the concerns and challenges that they have without attempting to "fix" these or offer strategies or solutions
- offer a straightforward and practical way to introduce the kinds of changes that are wanted by parents and carers

PCAP offers parents and carers the relational context, tools, ideas, resources and support that are universally needed to ensure the best outcomes for children.

PCAP has been designed to adapt to a wide range of cultural and developmental needs, making it suitable for many family situations and contexts. It is currently active in the UK, Ireland, Thailand, India, Singapore, Indonesia, South Africa and Kenya in a range of public and private settings.

This relatively short-term method is cost-effective and resource-light, and equips parents and carers with three essential skills that are learned and practised with the help of the PCAP practitioner. Early weeks see the parent/carer work only with the practitioner to enjoy these new ideas. When the parent/carer is ready, she introduces these skills to the child through a short weekly playtime that they share together. The PCAP practitioner does not work directly with the child unless necessary. This is to avoid undermining the parent/carer as the expert in her child's care. During the playtime, the child enjoys a "mini-kit" that has been put together by the parent/carer with the help of the PCAP practitioner. This kit contains some toys or alternative enjoyable activities that the child is known to like. It comes in a recycled shoebox or bag that is attractive for the individual child. This playtime ideally happens in the family home but can also be facilitated in other venues, for example the child's school or an agency or community setting.

As the home playtimes become an established part of family life, and the parent/carer enjoys seeing her new skills in action, the PCAP practitioner helps the parent/carer to roll them out into problematic areas of family life. There are often trigger times and behaviours that are very hard for families to manage, and the PCAP skills can be transferred to these times outside of the playtime. As the parent's or carer's confidence grows, the practitioner gently reduces her contact with the family to phone calls and text messages, until eventually the family is able to navigate everyday challenges with confidence.

In many cases, the family still has access to the PCAP practitioner for an agreed period to support parents and carers to embed the new relational culture within the family.

What is the theory and evidence base for Parent-Child Attachment Play?

PCAP is positioned squarely within attachment theory and, more specifically, within recent findings concerning how parents and carers activate a secure attachment relationship with their child.

Attachment theory is a well-established developmental and evolutionary theory explaining how the child uses proximity-seeking behaviours to keep the adult who cares for her readily available to meet her needs. This adult, who in attachment terms is known as the primary attachment figure, behaves in particular ways in response to the needs of the child. In turn, the child internalises a dynamic map or internal working model of what she has come to expect from this relationship (Bowlby, 1969).

Parental behaviour of course ranges in its sensitivity, warmth and consistency of response to the child. Whilst many practitioners are familiar with the tenets of attachment theory, I would like to explore them here through the child's voice and experiences. This helps ground a theoretical understanding of attachment in the moment-to-moment experience of the many children we may come across. It also helps to remind us that the varied attachment strategies that children develop are not readily under their control. Instead, children make a pragmatic attachment response to the behaviour of their primary attachment figure – including the good, bad and ugly.

There are four classic attachment styles which describe the relational strategies developed by children. These are shown reliably in testing after the age of one year through the use of the Strange Situation protocol (Ainsworth et al., 1978; Main and Solomon, 1990). Attachment styles are expressed along two domains – organisation and security – and are outlined below.

Organised and secure

This child experiences relatively consistent and "good-enough" care that meets her needs adequately and contingently. This includes the provision of emotional and physical safety. The child's distress is calmed sufficiently, her neurological and hormonal systems quieten and, over a relatively brief period, the child returns to equilibrium. This positive relational experience is internalised and optimised via a dynamic internal working model of attachment within the child. Just over 60% of the general population enjoys one secure attachment relationship with a primary attachment figure (Andreassen and West, 2007; van Izjendoorn et al., 1999). If the securely-attached child was able to verbalise how this relationship feels, she might say something like:

> *When you come to me, I feel much better and the overwhelming feelings I have are not so bad. You help me get through them and I realise that they pass. I am making sense of them. I can rely on you as my secure base. When I am with you, I feel safe. I am curious, and eager to explore the world. If something bad happens or I feel stressed, I can return to you and touch base and you make everything feel OK again.*

Organised and insecure (anxious/resistant)

This child does not experience reliable and consistent responses from her parent/carer. She has learned, over time, to dis/mistrust her. The child has learned to up-regulate under stress in order to ensure that her parent/carer becomes available to meet her needs.

However, this child is also ambivalent towards or even rejecting of her parent/carer owing to the lack of trust. Around 9% of the general population falls into this category (van Izjendoorn et al., 1999). Whilst this attachment style is less than optimal, it is still functional. However, it is associated with anxiety and passive withdrawn behaviours going forward across the lifespan (Greenberg, 1999; Weinfield et al., 1999). An attempt to put this style into the voice of the child might sound like:

> *I like to be close to you but am not too sure about the response I am going to get. Sometimes, I need to make a big fuss to get your attention but then, when you finally come, I am still not sure of you. I push you away. You get mad at me. I can't trust you. I spend much of my time feeling anxious and stressed. I can't depend on you.*

Organised and insecure (avoidant)

Here, once again, the child is not able to trust and rely on her attachment figure sufficiently to develop a secure attachment. Instead, she has learned that if she asks for her needs to be met, she is regularly ignored and rejected. Over time, this child learns not to voice her needs. Instead, she learns worrying strategies attempting to manage her own stress. Around 15% of the general population is thought to be in this category (van Ijzendoorn et al., 1999). Although functional, avoidant attachments are linked to aggressive and anti-social behaviours and negative affect over the lifespan (Egeland and Carlson, 2004; Suess et al., 1992; Weinfield et al., 1999). This child might say:

> *I love you but have learned that you only love me when I make no demands of you. Any big or scary feelings I have must be pushed down inside me. Or I can make myself numb so I can't feel them anymore. I must be strong on my own. I must be quiet, easy and good or you will reject me. Sometimes, I feel like I am going to explode with all these pushed-down feelings.*

Disorganised

This child is at the greatest risk of all and has not been able to form an organised attachment of any kind, whether secure or either of the insecure types. This child's experiences of her primary attachment figure are so frightening or overwhelming that it is impossible to internalise a working model of attachment at all (Main and Solomon, 1986). It has been shown that some 15% of the general population fall into this category (van Ijzendoorn et al., 1999). This attachment type is strongly linked to childhood abuse and future outcomes which are extremely poor (Egeland and Carlson, 2004; Greenberg, 1999).

Giving voice to this child is to enter a world of distress, fear and unbearable feelings. In fact, it is hard to verbalise at all:

> *Don't touch me ... stay away from me ... I am on constant alert, constantly terrified, watching, waiting, fearing, dreading. I trust no one and feel abandoned and rejected, with a pain so deep I cannot even name it. My extreme behaviour makes everyone hate and reject me and I get involved with all the wrong people looking for something to make me feel better ...*

Each of the four attachment styles is represented below in Figure 1.2 and shown across the two domains; organisation and security. The approximate spread of attachment styles across the general population is also indicated.

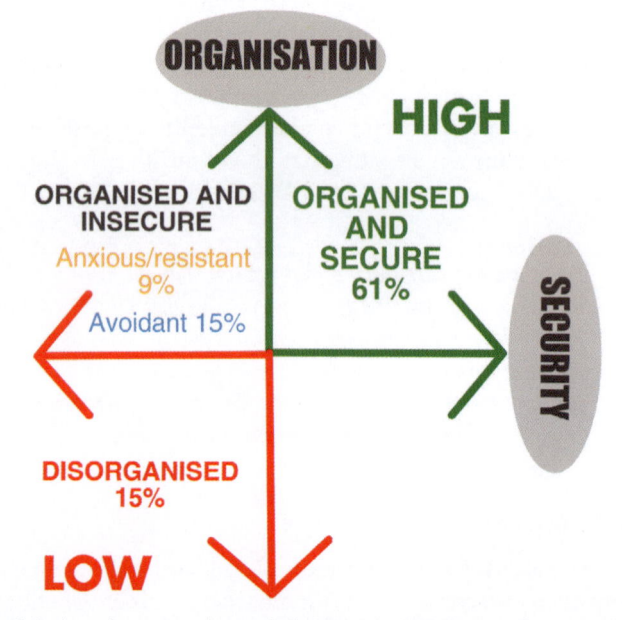

Figure 1.2: Attachment styles and their approximate spread across the general population

It is not hard to extrapolate forward which of the four children above is likely to be happier and healthier. Strengthening attachment security in the parent-child relationship is likely to have considerable positive impact across a number of areas of concern to those who work with families.

However, the ways in which attachment security is generated or operationalised in the parent-child relationship have puzzled attachment researchers until recently. The typical characteristics of parents and carers with securely-attached children have been known for a considerable time. These parents and carers are generally sensitive towards their children. However, the relative influence of parental sensitivity has been shown to be problematic in attachment studies (see, for example, Beckwith et al., 1999). Other active mechanisms are likely to be at work and have remained poorly understood.

In the 1990s, Peter Fonagy and his colleagues introduced the construct of Reflective Functioning (hereafter generally referred to as RF) as the ability or capacity to understand human behaviour in terms of underlying mental states and intentions. Through this understanding of mental states – intentions, feelings, thoughts, desires and beliefs – human beings begin to make sense of each other and make accurate predictions about behaviour and feelings (Fonagy and Target, 1997; Fonagy et al., 1991; Fonagy et al., 2004).

Later, Arietta Slade and her colleagues expanded the construct of RF to parental narratives about the ongoing parent-child relationship (Grienenberger et al., 2005; Slade et al., 2005a; Slade, 2005). A parent with sufficient RF can hold her child in mind; tune in to her thoughts and feelings; realise the separation between the child's thoughts and feelings and her own; enable her to understand that her thoughts and feelings and those of the child are intertwined and in interplay; and let the child know that she is understood in multiple ways (Maskell-Graham, 2016). Importantly, this parental ability or capacity seems to operate on a sliding scale.

In addition, a non-verbal measure of RF capacity called Parental Embodied Mentalising (PEM) has been developed (Shai, 2010). This can be seen and measured as the parent's ability to understand the child's mind-states from her whole-body expressions and to respond with her own kinaesthetic expressions. Thus, RF also has a non-verbal component which can be seen in the embodied interactions between parent and child (Shai and Belsky, 2011).

Adequate or sufficient parental RF capacity is associated with secure attachment in children (Slade, 2006). As we saw earlier, this security correlates with self-control and regulation, social competence, cognitive ability and school-readiness (Rispoli et al., 2013). Importantly, it is also associated with adaptive mentalisation processes (Fonagy and Target, 1997).

In addition, parental RF also has a protective function in the parent-child relationship. The development of a secure attachment occurs in those children whose parent/carer is either securely attached herself or who has enough RF for her own insecure patterns and behaviours to be successfully recognised and mediated (Slade et al., 2005b). In this respect, RF can function as a mechanism, catalyst or change agent in the transmission of attachment down the generations.

The exciting news for practitioners is that RF has been shown to be a skill or capacity that can be improved in many parents and carers. A raft of intervention studies show RF increases across a wide range of population groups: parents and carers attending universal or psycho-educational programmes (Kalland et al., 2016); those suffering from past trauma and domestic violence (Kearney and Cushing, 2012; Schechter et al., 2006; Stern, 2014); foster carers and adoptive parents (Bammens et al., 2015); parents in prison (Baradon et al., 2008; Sleed et al., 2013); and parents and carers in recovery from drug and alcohol misuse (Pajulo et al., 2006, 2012; Sadler et al., 2006; Söderström and Skårderud, 2009; Suchman et al., 2010). RF increases have also been shown in those carers providing early childcare (Tomlin et al., 2009).

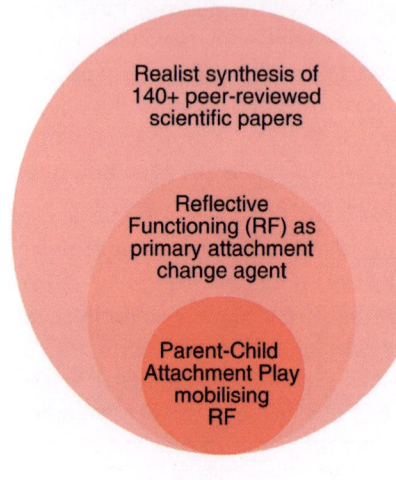

Figure 1.3: PCAP's theoretical and empirical basis

During the development of the PCAP method, a Realist synthesis of more than 140 peer-reviewed academic papers relating to RF theory and intervention was carried out (Pawson and Tilley, 1997). This revealed a robust correlation between improved parental RF and secure attachment in children. Not only this, the studies showed that RF itself could be measured on a sliding scale. Sufficiency of parental RF showed good results. In other words, parents and carers do not need high levels of RF, but they do need adequate or sufficient RF. PCAP has been designed as a means to develop adequacy of parental RF which, in turn, is known to strengthen the quality of the parent-child attachment relationship. Given that the papers studied for the development of PCAP include positive increases in RF for families with complex needs, it is likely that PCAP can be used confidently with a range of families. The timing of this offer is likely to be a critical factor.

What are the ten steps of Parent-Child Attachment Play?

The ten steps are outlined here and presented in full in a detailed case study in Part 2. Having a series of steps – rather than a set number of weeks – allows PCAP practitioners to lengthen or shorten the duration of the method as appropriate, depending on parental need.

1. Referral and establishment of the practitioner-parent relationship, including listening to the parent/carer's relationship "story" and setting up weekly meetings
2. Assessment of need and goal-setting
3. Learning and practising Skill 1: Play – preparing the mini-kit
4. Learning and practising Skill 2: Containment
5. Plan parent-child home playtimes and review progress
6. Learning and practising Skill 3: Reflective Functioning (Head, Heart and Hands)
7. "You and Me" playtimes begin at home between parent/carer and child
8. Roll out playtime skills to everyday family life

9. Change to phone/text/email-only support
10. Endings and celebrations (reporting)

What are the three skills that parents and carers develop in Parent-Child Attachment Play?

The three PCAP skills shared with parents and carers are:

1. Play
2. Containment
3. Reflective Functioning (Head, Heart and Hands)

As we saw earlier, play is the means or modality through which Reflective Functioning is practised, and containment provides the safe space in which RF can flourish. They are the essential and operational components of the PCAP method.

The three skills are shared with parents and carers in the following pattern:

1. Skill is introduced and explored through discussion and creative activities
2. Practitioner demonstrates the skill with the parent/carer so that she can experience it for herself
3. Discussion and reflection
4. Parent/carer practises the skill with the practitioner
5. Discussion and reflection
6. Practitioner gives the parent/carer some insight into how she might make a child feel by using the skill – the child is given a voice in the learning of the skills between practitioner and parent/carer

Skill 1: Play

Play is the means by which parents and carers practise, with their child, the operational attachment mechanism built into PCAP. There are many types of play, and the best way to describe the play used in PCAP is "child-oriented". Child-oriented play is the type of play which best meets the needs of the individual child. It can take many shapes and forms – for example, free play, creative play, imaginary play, shared play and structured play. Where possible, creative and imaginary activity is encouraged. However, PCAP can also include alternative activities, particularly for teenagers, including electronic or technology-based games. The key principle is that parents and carers think carefully about the preferences and needs of their individual child and provide for this appropriately. One child may like make-believe and fantasy play involving action figures and games of battles, whilst another may like ritualistic play and prefer only limited types of toys or games, and another may have restricted mobility and enjoy supported sensory activities. In this step of the PCAP process, parents and carers are encouraged as the experts in knowing what their child prefers and generating ideas about how to provide this. Practitioners can use open questions and make helpful suggestions to support this.

Child-oriented play also allows the play provision to adapt to cultural factors – for example, games and toys which reflect and respect the culture and traditions of the family. Traditions in one community will be inappropriate in another, and the world-view of the practitioner must be considered and circumvented as required.

In cases where the parent/carer finds it harder to provide playful opportunities with and for her child, the practitioner finds playful strengths in the parent/carer and begins from there. Practitioner and parent/carer may enjoy simple activities together, such as noughts and crosses or other culturally-appropriate games. The practitioner may ask the parent/carer if she remembers any games or activities that she enjoyed as a child. This is done with care and reference to the parent/carer's own history. For example, a parent/carer whose own childhood was very difficult will not benefit from using reminiscence and personal experiences. The practitioner and parent/carer may also make some creative items together. For example, they could enjoy making a sensory toy from a recycled clear bottle filled with water and glitter, or tie recycled gift ribbons and plastic strips to a wooden curtain ring or hair scrunchie to make a streamer toy.

The PCAP practitioner provides enjoyable activities for the parent/carer to experience. This shared space allows the parent/carer to enjoy quality time with a trusted practitioner. Whether chatty or quiet, the parent/carer can enjoy being in a supportive and reflective relationship with the practitioner.

This embodies key principles of PCAP: "being with" parents and carers rather than "doing to", and giving sufficient space for the parent/carer to develop confidence and strengths from the inside out. Practitioners have available to them access to a number of online resources about play and its importance to child development. These can be used as handouts or supporting material with parents and carers where appropriate.

Once parents and carers are comfortable with the idea of play, they have a chance to experience it for themselves. The practitioner facilitates a ten-minute playtime with the parent using a simple box or bag of resources. If ten minutes is too long, the practitioner can shorten it as needed. This might look a little like:

> Practitioner: *OK, it's time to have a try at the play! Please imagine that you are a child looking in this box of toys for the first time. Please take them out and explore them. You are in charge of the play and I follow your lead. I'll help if you ask me to, but won't take over. OK?*

The practitioner lets the parent/carer know when five minutes and then one minute remains, and also when it is time to end the play.

Vitally, the parent/carer must only ever imagine being *a* child. To become *their own* child will activate all of the difficulties and complexities of the relationship between them. To become themselves as a child will activate all the complexities and processes of their own child-state and childhood history. Subsequent feelings and conversations from both of the above would potentially come under the domain of counselling and psychotherapy. PCAP practitioners are generally not adult counsellors or psychotherapists (although they could be). Instead, any thoughts and feelings that do come up for parents and carers through the PCAP method are validated and contained through the practitioner's own use of the attachment mechanism, RF. Onward referrals can be made when

An overview of Parent-Child Attachment Play

a PCAP practitioner feels that a parent/carer would benefit from individual counselling or other types of help before continuning with PCAP.

After the parent/carer has experienced the play, the practitioner asks her how she found the experience – "How was that?" As the parent/carer responds, the PCAP practitioner uses her own RF skills to tune into the thoughts and feelings of the parent/carer. She lets her know that she is understood. The practitioner does not try to fix things or suggest solutions. Through RF, the parent/carer will begin to feel safe and secure in the practitioner-parent relationship and can be gently helped to find her own answers.

The parent/carer then has her turn at facilitating a short playtime and the practitioner takes the role of a child. At the end of this, the same question is asked – "How was that?" Discussion and reflections follow. Finally, the practitioner gives the parent/carer some insight into how a child may feel about having this unique time with a parent/carer. This is a powerful part of the skill-sharing process. For example, the practitioner can say something like:

> *I really liked having you all to myself! You didn't even check your phone! It makes me feel important when you spend this time with me. Can we do it again?*

The final part of the play skill is for the practitioner to support the parent/carer to make a mini-kit of playful toys or activities that she thinks best represents the preferences and needs of her child or teenager. These toys and activities do not have to be new but they must be new to the child. Nothing must be taken from the child's existing toys because these belong to her and are already loaded with ownership, metaphor and meaning for the child.

A recycled shoebox or robust bag makes a good container for this playtime mini-kit. The kit is kept containable and contained so that the parent/carer feels able to manage it. My experiences with families have shown that parents and carers may find the prospect of providing both a playtime and some toys/activities for their child overwhelming. Many parents and carers may also find that the prospect of mess and playful activity brings anxiety and a feeling of being out of control of their usual family domain. Keeping the playtime relatively short and the PCAP mini-kit manageable, contained and easy to put away has been very helpful for parents and carers.

Some examples of mini-kits put together around the globe include:

1. Recycled shoebox filled with a selection of toys and creative materials: paper, pens, crayons, safety scissors, tape, craft items, toy figures, animals, dinosaurs, sea creatures and small items of toy furniture, a bag of crystals and shells
2. Recycled large gift box filled with pieces of Lego®, a Lego board and accessories
3. Plastic tub filled with locally-sourced wooden figures and animals, various pieces of material and home-made instruments
4. Drawstring bag filled with a few structured games (Uno®, trump cards and playing cards), and pens and paper for other games (noughts and crosses, hangman, etc.)
5. Shoebox filled with paper, pens, crayons, stickers, pipecleaners, craft materials, recycled items, safety scissors, tape for making "things"
6. Harry Potter-themed bag – action figures, potential dressing-up masks and capes, beast drawings to make and colour, wands, pretend ingredients for "spells", themed stickers and cards
7. Shoebox filled with nail polishes, nail stickers, hand cream, nail file, varnish remover
8. Shoebox filled with finger- and stick-puppets and materials to make more puppet characters, plus a piece of fabric, wallpaper offcuts and other recycled materials – fabric could go over the shoebox to become the puppet theatre, whilst wallpaper and other materials provide potential for backdrops and other props
9. Recycled shoebox filled with a kit to make a model plane and accessories
10. Bag of model soldiers/warriors/superheroes to play with, recycled materials to make scenery/castles/spaceships etc., and other accessories for stories, missions and battles

An overview of Parent-Child Attachment Play

Figure 1.4: An example of a mini-kit

Mini-kits also need to reflect the developmental needs of the individual child and be designed at a level that promotes engagement and enjoyment. Parents and carers are given a fairly low limit on what they can spend to create it (I have a limit of £5 for new items). This makes the box affordable for most families and avoids some parents and carers spending an unnecessarily large sum of money. "Pound shops", bargain shops and charity shops are a good source of the kinds of item often needed. PCAP practitioners also encourage the use of everyday and recycled items that are safe for play use.

The PCAP practitioner supports the parent/carer to make the kit and, where new ideas might be needed, uses open questions to help the parent/carer think about what might work well. Where parents and carers need extra support to provide a mini-kit for a range of reasons including economic ones, practitioners can provide a range of potential materials and ideas for them to choose from – a mini-shop, if you like.

Practitioners, parents and carers are often worried about children's perceived preference for electronic toys and hand-held devices and tablets. In PCAP, there is no perceived hierarchy of "better" or "worse" toys and/or activities. Rather, it is ideal if the toys, games and activities that parents and carers provide can potentially create parent-child interaction.

I find that children and teenagers are very accepting of the idea that the play that parents and carers offer at home for PCAP is "different" and, generally, not electronic. Helping parents and carers to think beyond electronic games to what the children are actually enjoying is helpful.

For example, many children and teens enjoy Lego Minecraft, a brick-based console adventure game released in 2012. There are two modes in the game, survival and creative. Players can construct anything and everything in the game's virtual environment out of Lego-shaped blocks of many things – for example sand, rock and lava. The ultimate aim of the game is to survive and build.

Parents and carers may come up with playful ideas inspired by the game and provide actual Lego, recycled materials, scissors, tape and materials to make characters and monsters, for example.

Where electronic games may be the only way for a parent/carer to be alongside her child, this is accepted. Play, in all its forms, can be the language of PCAP. There are some great games which promote interaction and enjoyment between parent/carer and child.

In addition, the child does not need imagination or even theory of mind to benefit from the PCAP approach – it is the *parental* RF capacity which is known to strengthen the parent-child relationship. Thus, it can be easily adapted for children with a range of specific additional needs, developmental difficulties and/or physical/learning disabilities.

Play skill summary

Introduce child-oriented play skill to parents and carers (see Appendices 4a and 4b)

Play simple games together to unlock playfulness and make a toy

Parent/carer tries out the play as a child – practitioner facilitates

Practitioner asks parent/carer: "How was that?" – discussion and reflections using RF

Practitioner plays as a child – parent/carer facilitates

Practitioner asks parent/carer: "How was that?" – discussion and reflections using RF

Practitioner gives insight to the parent/carer about how a child might feel: for example, "I felt important because you played with me, I liked having you all to myself"

Make a mini-kit ready for "You and Me" playtimes at home

Skill 2: Containment

The containment skill in PCAP is best described as the ability of one person to make another feel safe and contained through words, action or touch, or through managing time, space and the wider environment. Containment is a useful and neutral way to help parents and carers think about boundaries, expectations, rules, behaviours and environments.

In PCAP multiple layers of containment are built in for both the practitioner-parent relationship and the parent-child relationship. Practitioners are mindful of the many ways in which they help create a safe physical and emotional space in which the parent or carer can thrive. From providing a regular meeting day and time to arranging an uninterrupted, comfortable and regular meeting space, from greeting the parent/carer at the door to sitting alongside them, and from practising RF skills during discussion and reflections to helping guide the parent/carer through the PCAP steps, the practitioner is helping the parent/carer to feel contained.

Containment facilitates sufficient thinking, feeling and reflective space in the parent/carer. When parental worries or anxieties take up all the space in the parent/carer's mind, there is no space left for RF to grow.

When the containment skill is transferred home, it helps the child to feel safe and secure in the knowledge that her parent/carer is taking care of her and taking responsibility for managing the home environment.

Containment is often a tough skill for families to implement. The benefit of PCAP is that it ring-fences a short time for the parent/carer to learn, practise and then implement containment at home. This makes it much more manageable. The transference of the containment skill is itself contained!

The PCAP practitioner introduces the idea of containment to the parent/carer and, through listening, reflecting and using open questions, gauges how the parent/carer feels about the idea. Some parents/carers are very relieved to find out that they are going to be encouraged to contain their children in a variety of ways during PCAP. Many are understandably worried that, by adopting a playful approach, they will somehow lose control over their child and their ability to control the situation and the child's behaviour.

Other parents are very concerned about containing their children owing to the conflict they associate with trying to do so. Over the years, I have met many parents and carers who want to enjoy a greater sense of control over their child's behaviour but generally feel out of control. They worry about being punitive and then accidentally find themselves becoming just that, through frustration and a sense of helplessness. Others want so much to be different from their own parents and yet find themselves acting out the very punitive measures they want to avoid. Added to this is a general message in society that parents/carers are to blame for children's poor behaviour. This traps parents/carers into a situation in which they cannot win. On the one hand, they want something different but cannot be honest about the level of difficulty they have at home because of the judgemental attitude towards parents and carers. Most, if not all, parents and carers have trouble with their children at times, which is shown in the huge interest in and market for parenting advice.

Unfortunately, not all parenting advice is theory-driven and evidence-based. As discussed earlier, PCAP is not a parenting approach because of the problematic nature of the "parenting" concept. It is a strengths-based relational approach. Where children enjoy a secure attachment with their parent/carer, helpful behaviours and positive outcomes generally follow across all domains.

Once parents/carers are comfortable with the idea of containment and their role in establishing this at home, PCAP practitioners help them set up a contained framework for the home-based play sessions.

First, the PCAP practitioner supports the parent/carer to think about the best day and time for the home play sessions (same day, same time, every week). The practitioner sows the seed that the playtime happens every week without fail, regardless of how things have been at home. The playtime is never withdrawn as a punishment for poor behaviour.

Further planning is often needed if there are other children in the family and there are no other family members to offer help. Difficulties with multiple siblings to manage, shift working patterns and partners working away are often common factors. In some instances, childcare for siblings can be organised where there is no additional support. Wherever possible, the PCAP playtimes take place at home so that the parent/carer can truly identify herself as the agent of change in her own domain.

However, it is sometimes necessary to help parents/carers facilitate the home-based playtimes at an alternative venue, for example the child's school. In Cape Town, South Africa, PCAP is used within a network of women's refuges and this is where the parent-child playtimes are hosted.

In other instances, a staggered approach to the home-based play is implemented. For example, the play sessions may begin at another venue (school, agency, clinic) and then move to the home once well-established. Another transitional strategy is for the PCAP practitioner to sit in on the home-based playtimes for the first couple of weeks until they are going well.

The second aspect of the containment skill is to help the parent/carer to identify a contained area or space in which the playtime can take place. This very much depends on the culture and setting of family life. Examples of contained spaces include: a large rug in a living space; the whole of a safe, small room; the kitchen table and chairs around it; a blanket spread out on the floor; and a large sofa. PCAP happens in many different places around the world, and what matters is the nature of the space rather than hard-and-fast rules about it. It must be quiet and uninterrupted, small enough to contain the child and large enough to allow play. Do not use bedrooms or the child's own room if she has one, but a neutral space. Outside spaces can be used if they are sufficiently contained.

Playtimes have a simple set of positive rules for the parent/carer and child to keep. The parent/carer is responsible for keeping the rules. At the beginning of each playtime, the parent/carer lets the child know these very sensible and reasonable rules and asks for her agreement to them:

1. We look after you
2. We look after me
3. We look after the box/bag of toys/activities
4. We stay in the space

An overview of Parent-Child Attachment Play

Many parent and carers are worried about remembering the rules, so we usually have some fun making a poster or card of them together. This is carried out with sensitivity towards literacy and language capability. Some parents and carers want to write things down, whilst others use visual signs or "emoji" icons. Figure 1.5 shows an example of a poster.

Figure 1.5: Example of PCAP rules poster

The value of making the PCAP rules together is two-fold; first, PCAP practitioners can create a reflective space in which to discuss the rules and listen to parents/carers whilst making the poster; and second, the making of the poster takes the rules from being an external idea to one which has been changed to belong to the parent/carer. For my work in the UK I have a laminating machine, and many parents/carers enjoy seeing how lamination creates a nice finish to their creations. I could even suggest that the lamination helps provide a sense of the rules being robust and able to last. The rules can be kept as part of the playtime mini-kit. Some parents and carers have suggested sticking them to the inside of the shoebox lid, which is a great idea.

Once the rules are established, practitioners help the parent/carer practise how to begin each playtime with her child. In our practice sessions, we may use a blanket on the floor or a table and chairs to represent the contained space. The mini-kit is placed ready on the table with the lid off and a few toys arranged to look inviting. Children are encouraged to use the toilet before the playtime begins. The practitioner demonstrates how to introduce each playtime:

> Practitioner: *OK, it's time for our "You and Me" playtime! We have 20 [or 30–40 minutes for older children] – no more, no less – and you can play however you like. We just have four rules to keep: we look after you, we look after me, we look after the toys, and we stay in the space. Great rules. Agreed? [Wait for agreement.] I'll let you know when we have five minutes left and then one minute left. Time to play!*

Of course, parents and carers (and most children and teenagers) want to know what happens if the rules get broken. PCAP practitioners share and demonstrate a non-punitive approach with parents and carers using child choices and consequences.

> Practitioner: *If the rules are broken, that's OK, that's your choice. You get a second chance to agree to our rules. If the rules are broken again, that's OK, that's your choice. You get a final chance. If the rules are broken a third time, that's OK, that's your choice and playtime will simply come to an end. We will play again next week, same day, same time.*

Parents/carers are often both excited and worried about the prospect of having a gentle and non-punitive way to contain their child's behavioural choices during the playtime. PCAP practitioners explore these concerns using their own RF and open questions. They also help parents and carers to practise what to say to their child if they choose to break the agreed rules. The rules are designed to cover a wide range of possible behavioural choices, and can be adapted depending on family culture. For example, some parents and carers may feel that swearing or bad language is not acceptable in their family home, so when their child or teenager asks if swearing or bad language is OK, parents and carers can ask that this is covered by the rules about looking after you and me and causing no offence. For other families, the use of certain language will not overly concern them. It is vital that the four playtime rules are sufficient and do not become too restrictive for the child or teenager whilst respecting reasonable concerns raised by the parent/carer.

If the rules are broken three times, the parent/carer remains neutral and calm. She is encouraged to use breathing and other regulatory ideas to help her manage her own potentially difficult feelings. Many parents and carers tell me that just having a set routine to follow helps them stay cool and calm.

The parent/carer acknowledges the child's choice to end, gently places the toys and/or activities back in the box, and puts it somewhere safe. If the child gets angry or upset, the parent/carer acknowledges that it is hard when our choices lead to things we don't like. She is kind and empathic and uses her growing RF skills. The parent/carer stays with the child and may suggest going to the kitchen for a drink. This can be helpful in sticking with the "choices and consequences" approach and in helping both parent/carer and child transition from difficult feelings of upset, anger or frustration to a neutral space. Poor behaviour, either outside or during the playtimes, is never punished by the removal of the play session. These continue every week on the same day and at the same time.

Containment skill summary

Introduce containment skill (see Appendices 5a and 5b)

Introduce playtime rules and make poster

Practitioner introduces rules to parent/carer as if she is a child

Practitioner asks parent/carer: "How was that?"

Parent/carer introduces rules to practitioner as if she is a child

Practitioner asks parent/carer: "How was that?"

Practitioner gives insight to the parent/carer about how a child might feel: for example, "I felt safe and relaxed because I know what was expected of me. I like the rules because they apply to both to us and they are easy to remember."

Practitioner introduces what happens if the rules get broken

Practitioner practises explaining to the parent/carer as if she is a child

Practitioner asks parent/carer: "How was that?"

Parent/carer introduces what happens if the rules get broken to practitioner as if she is a child

Practitioner asks parent/carer: "How was that?"

Practitioner gives insight to the parent/carer about how a child might feel: for example, "I feel safe because you are in charge. I like that the rules are consistent and fair and you explained them clearly. I know where I stand and can trust you."

Practitioner introduces the idea of helping to contain the ending of the playtime by giving the child five-minute and one-minute warnings or "heads-up"

Practitioner supports parent/carer to identify a regular time (same day, same time, each week) for the home-based playtime and a contained space in which it can happen

An overview of Parent-Child Attachment Play

Skill 3: Head, Heart and Hands (Reflective Functioning)

Earlier, we looked at attachment theory and research and saw how recent advances have identified an important attachment-generative mechanism, Reflective Functioning (RF). RF is the main attachment mechanism used in PCAP and has been turned into a parent-friendly tool for parents/carers to learn and practise with their children. This is illustrated in Figure 1.6.

HEAD, HEART AND HANDS

Head: us as parents focusing on our child and thinking about her and her thoughts – seeing the world though her eyes and from her point of view and understanding that her thoughts, ideas and intentions are separate from ours; us as parents knowing and recognising that our own thoughts can be affected by our child's thoughts and vice versa in complicated and sometimes painful ways

Heart: us as parents putting ourselves inside our child and feeling her feelings – feeling what it is like for her – realising that her feelings are separate from ours; recognising our own feelings and responses to our child; knowing that our child's feelings can affect our feelings and vice versa in complicated and sometimes painful ways

Hands: in reponse to thinking and feeling, us as parents doing and saying things to let our child know that we are trying to understand her – acknowledging that her individual thoughts and feelings are respected as separate from ours (guessing is good because it is hard to mind-read!); understanding that our thoughts and feelings affect our children's and the quality of our interactions with them, again in complicated in sometimes painful ways

Figure 1.6: Reflective Functioning as Head, Heart and Hands

Head, Heart and Hands is shared with parents/carers as the third skill in PCAP. An explanation is given together with a parent-friendly card – available to download from the online resource bank. One of the card options is designed to be turned into a fridge- or mirror-magnet. The other is credit card-sized and designed for pockets in purses, wallets and mobile phone cases.

Simple and playful activities between the practitioner and the parent/carer allow the Head, Heart and Hands concepts to come to life. For example, a series of expressive face shots of children and teenagers are looked at. The pictures have empty "thought bubbles" around them. The practitioner and parent/carer have fun making up the best thoughts to match each face. Of course, there are many possibilities! This is a chance for parents/carers to realise that RF is about tuning in to their child's thoughts and feelings, and sometimes having to guess. Guessing is good because actual mind-reading is pretty difficult!

Once parents/carers are comfortable with the concept, they practise using Head, Heart and Hands with the practitioner. It is ideal to split this into separate practice sessions for Head (thoughts), Heart (feelings) and Hands (verbal and non-verbal expressions of understanding towards the child). First, the practitioner asks the parent/carer to play once again with the mini-kit for ten minutes. She explains that during this time she is going to think only of the parent/carer. If other thoughts come into her mind, she is going to acknowledge them and then return to hold the parent/carer in mind.

> Practitioner: *OK. Let's give this a try. Can you play with the mini-kit once again, for ten minutes ... as if you are a child? Whilst you are playing, I am going to hold you in mind and keep coming back to you if my mind wanders or I accidentally think of something else. It's hard, so I am going to concentrate! Ready?*

The practitioner lets the parent/carer know when five minutes remain, and then one minute, and then brings the play to a close. The practitioner asks the parent/carer how it felt to be playing with someone holding them in mind. Responses are usually mixed, and the practitioner uses her own RF to let the parent/carer know that she is understood. I am regularly heard to say things like, "Yes, it is a bit weird, you're right".

As with the other skills, it is now the parent/carer's turn to practise holding the practitioner in mind as if she was a child. When the practice play is over, more discussions follow as the parent/carer explores how they felt about holding the practitioner in mind. The practitioner also gives a voice to how a child might feel enjoying the full and undivided attention of her parent/carer.

This process is then repeated, with the practitioner giving the parent/carer an experience of playing with someone really trying to tune in to their feelings during the play.

> Practitioner: *This time can you play as a child again and I am going to see if I can tune in to your feelings. I will watch closely and see if I can feel what you are feeling. I will also have a good guess if I am not completely sure – it doesn't have to be perfect.*

The practitioner is very attentive to the internal states and external behaviours of the parent/carer during this practice. Discussion follows, with the practitioner asking the parent/carer how it felt to have someone trying to attune to their feelings. As before, the practitioner uses her own RF during this discussion.

The parent/carer then practises on the practitioner, and it is very helpful for the practitioner to make her feelings fairly obvious for the parent/carer. Discussion follows once again. Finally, in this section, the practitioner gives the parent/carer insight into how a child might feel playing with an adult who is really trying to understand how she is feeling from moment to moment.

So far, the practitioner and parent/carer have arguably been developing their empathy skills. However, RF takes empathy further and asks that the parent/carer recognises that her thoughts and feelings are separate from the child's but are linked and in interplay with them. RF also asks parents/carers to communicate to the child their understanding of her in verbal and non-verbal ways. In turn, this effort activates or mechanises a secure attachment response in the child.

The practitioner introduces the final idea of doing or saying something that lets the child know that she is understood. The practitioner also emphasises that guessing is fine.

> Practitioner: *OK! This time can you play as a child and I am going to hold you in mind and try to tune in to your thoughts and feelings. A few times, I am going to let you know that I get it*

– that I understand you – I might have to guess, but that's OK. I'm going to use my expressions and body language. If I do say anything, it is going to be a short statement. Let's have a go!

Discussion follows this, and parents/carers often say that they feel unsure. The practitioner reassures them that the research says that we only need to be "adequate" at RF – which is a relief for many. The practitioner also emphasises that the parent/carer knows her child and will be getting better and better at noticing what is going on for her – this is a skill that gets better with practice.

The parent/carer then practises on the practitioner, who is careful to create opportunities in the play for the parent/carer to try a verbal or non-verbal response. Discussion allows for the practitioner to support the parent/carer. The practitioner also gives the parent/carer insight into how these verbal and non-verbal reflections activate a feeling of safety and security in the child.

This skill benefits from additional games and activities which bring the concepts to life and help the parent/carer to grow in skill and confidence. Some parents have even been known to request further information on RF and attachment. Practitioners have access to some suggested resources in the online resource bank which accompanies this method.

Reflective Functioning skill summary

Introduce Head, Heart and Hands (RF) skill (see Appendices 6a and 6b)

Introduce Head idea – holding a child in mind

Parent/carer plays as a child – practitioner facilitates and holds the parent/carer in mind

Practitioner asks parent/carer: "How was that?" – discussion and reflections using RF

Practitioner plays as a child – parent/carer facilitates and holds the practitioner in mind

Practitioner asks parent/carer: "How was that?" – discussion and reflections using RF

Practitioner gives insight to the parent/carer about how a child might feel: for example, "I can feel you with me. You're not thinking about other things like work or jobs to do … you are focused on me and I really like that".

Introduce Heart idea – trying to tune in and feel what the child is feeling

Parent/carer plays as a child – practitioner facilitates and tunes in to the parent/carer's feelings during the play

Practitioner asks parent/carer: "How was that?" – discussion and reflections using RF

Practitioner plays as a child – parent/carer facilitates and tunes in to the practitioner's feelings during the play

Practitioner asks parent/carer: "How was that?" – discussion and reflections using RF

Practitioner gives insight to the parent/carer about how a child might feel: for example, "When I was feeling frustrated because I couldn't get the dinosaur in the little box, you were right by me and felt my frustration. I felt seen, I felt better …"

Introduce Hands idea – verbal and non-verbal ways of letting the child know that she is understood in multiple ways

Parent/carer plays as a child – practitioner facilitates and says and does a few things to show the parent/carer that she is understood

Practitioner asks parent/carer: "How was that?" – discussion and reflections using RF

Practitioner plays as a child – parent/carer facilitates and practises doing and saying a few things to show the child that she is understood

Practitioner asks parent/carer: "How was that?" – discussion and reflections using RF

Practitioner gives insight to the parent/carer about how a child might feel: for example, "When I got excited about that game and you grinned at me, I felt safe with you. You also got it when I couldn't tie that string up and wanted to give up. You got it that I was really upset, even though it was just a silly bit of string. I feel secure with you. I can trust you."

Where does the skill-sharing method for Parent-Child Attachment Play originate?

The PCAP method has been informed by elements of the skill transference model in Filial Therapy originally developed by Drs Louise and Bernard Guerney and, more recently, by Dr Risë vanFleet.

Filial Therapy was developed in the 1960s by the Guerneys as a treatment for children with social, emotional and behavioural problems (Guerney and Ryan, 2013). It uses a psycho-educational framework to teach parents in the use of therapeutic play skills with their children. Filial Therapy is well-established in North America and continues to grow worldwide. It provides a combination of affective, behavioural and cognitive methods of therapy in which children are supported via their parents/carers acting as the facilitators.

Bernard Guerney developed Filial Therapy as an alternative to the assumption that it was parental pathology that largely caused children's psycho-social and behavioural problems. Instead, he looked more at the lack of synchrony in the parent-child relationship (ibid.). He sought to create an intervention which equipped parents with the necessary knowledge and skills to improve the quality of parent-child interactions.

As a practising play therapist, Guerney proposed the idea of teaching the basic skills of the play therapist to parents. Parents learn four skills with the Filial Therapist: structuring, empathic listening, child-centred imaginary play and limit-setting. The goal is to eliminate the presenting problems within the parent-child relationship at their source, develop positive interactions between parents and children, and increase families' communication, coping and problem-solving skills moving forward (vanFleet, 2014). Filial Therapy has been shown to be effective as part of a recent meta-analytic review of Child-Centred Play Therapy (Lin and Bratton, 2015). Filial Therapy is a comprehensive and specialised play therapy technique and is highly recommended for practitioner training.

PCAP was inspired by the skill transference model used in Filial Therapy. Using just a single attachment-generative mechanism and the reduction of internal and external stressors on the parent/carer makes the PCAP method accessible to a wide range of practitioners with the necessary experience of direct family work.

Which parents/carers is Parent-Child Attachment Play for?

This method can be used with a wide range of families, either as a stand-alone method or as part of a pathway of support. It is best seen as an early intervention method designed to offer support before the family situation escalates to a very serious level or as a follow-up approach where a more intensive intervention has settled the relational difficulties.

Generally, it works well with families in which the parent-child relationship is under strain and/or child behaviours are a cause for concern. This includes using PCAP as part of the fostering and adoptive processes to support the establishment or stabilisation of secure attachment relationships in the context of a disrupted attachment history.

Whilst PCAP is not immediately suitable for parents/carers whose family life is in crisis or who have highly complex needs which are ongoing – for example, substance misuse or mental health difficulties – it may be appropriate later in the overall process. Consequently, specialist services may be offered first and, when the situation is more stable, followed with PCAP provision.

The pathway idea also allows for PCAP to be used as a universal health promotion strategy to help strengthen the parent-child relationship and protect against known risk factors at work. Prevention is better (and cheaper) than cure, and the benefits of secure attachment are well-documented and proven. As we saw earlier, all families struggle at times with their relationships with their child(ren), and support information is varied in its quality and evidence base. PCAP can be packaged in different ways to suit a range of audiences and budgets. The multiple ways of delivering PCAP are outlined later in this Part.

How do I know that Parent-Child Attachment Play works?

The PCAP method is built on a large body of peer-reviewed research showing the transformative impact of the attachment-generative mechanism, RF, on the quality of the parent-child relationship. A synthesis of more than 140 published papers looking at RF reveals it as the primary generative mechanism, with a number of other key mechanisms in a supportive role. These mechanisms are explicitly activated and nurtured in the PCAP skills and ten-step process. Whilst derived from this evidence base, PCAP itself is a relatively new method and in the early stages of building an evidence base of its own. A number of university studies have been completed or are currently underway to evaluate the impact of PCAP in a range of settings. A series of practitioner case studies from around the globe is also being compiled. The ongoing findings are regularly updated and available in the online resource bank.

Can Parent-Child Attachment Play be used in different formats?

PCAP can be configured differently according to family needs and resource availability. Various formats are possible, including:

- One-to-one work with the parent/carer and PCAP practitioner meeting in an agency or community setting
- One-to-one work with the parent/carer and PCAP practitioner meeting in the family home
- PCAP practitioner working with both parents/carers at the same time
- PCAP practitioner working with both parents/carers separately, for example, where parents are separated or divorced and unable to work together
- PCAP practitioner running a small group for parents/carers in an agency, clinical, educational or community setting

- PCAP practitioners sharing the three skills with parents/carers as part of their ongoing relationship and work with the family
- PCAP practitioners turning the three skills into a short series of workshops for parents/carers
- PCAP practitioners using PCAP to enhance the skills of secondary attachment figures, for example extended family, teaching assistants, childminders and nursery staff.

The level of need should ideally drive the design of the PCAP method in the varying circumstances, but the reality is that resources are often stretched. If the frequency and intensity of PCAP provision is too low, it will not generate the level of agency needed in the parent/carer. It may even set parents/carers up to fail.

In addition, commissioners and practitioners need to consider how best to ensure retention, particularly in cases of more complex need. It is likely that some of the families most likely to enjoy and benefit from PCAP are the very ones who may struggle to attend a venue outside the home. Home-based PCAP provision may result in a more consistent and reliable process. For some PCAP practitioners, home visiting will already be an established part of their work. For others, it may be possible (with the right policies and procedures in place) to offer home-based provision, or there may be another venue very close by that would support and maximise attendance and retention.

How long does the Parent-Child Attachment Play method take?

The length of the method varies, depending on a number of factors. The ten steps can represent a similar number of weeks, or considerably longer. My longest PCAP relationship was with an adoptive parent and lasted for 18 weeks (over a six-month period). Individual sessions lasted for approximately one hour. My shortest has been sharing the PCAP skills with a couple in my office for two hours! Both yielded positive results, which were maintained on being followed-up six months later. These examples are useful because they reflect the potential level of family complexity and need.

An adoptive mother beginning a new relationship with an older child with complex relational history and needs is a very different scenario to a family with minor difficulties. Frequency and intensity are key factors in providing sustainable results. Most PCAP provision falls between these examples, and allowing 12–14 hours for the full PCAP method is likely to generate positive results.

Sharing the three skills with groups of parents/carers in a workshop-style environment will take just a few weeks or sessions. The workshop approach is a favourite of mine and works well as a universal health promotion tactic, for example in a school setting where parents/carers are invited to a short series of PCAP workshops.

In Mumbai, India, parents/carers attended a weekend workshop along with interested practitioners. They enjoyed the three skills, created a mini-kit and began playtimes at home with their child(ren). Ongoing email support was on offer following the workshop. The following is an anonymised quote from one of the parents (a mother of two young boys) who emailed me for support with the subsequent process and gave me permission to share its impact:

> *We go about our lives with our children, but this time is devoted to my child and me. I think it has helped me to read my child better. What he likes and doesn't like. This has happened because I have "been" with my child and not just sat beside him.*

How much does Parent-Child Attachment Play cost to deliver?

The main cost of PCAP is the practitioner and her professional time. Additional costs may include venue hire, resources and the initial mentoring from another experienced PCAP practitioner. Small groups are more cost-effective and larger workshop groups are the cheapest model. Parental need must be balanced with economic factors, as a mismatch will result in a failure to deliver positive outcomes for families.

An additional cost is a small licence fee for using the method and online resource bank. This is kept as low as possible and is used to update and maintain practitioner resources, develop online tools for

PCAP practitioners and revise the PCAP method in the light of new research findings.

Can Parent-Child Attachment Play be delivered privately?

PCAP is being used in many countries around the world. PCAP practitioners may be employed or may volunteer to deliver direct work with families. PCAP can be added to their existing toolkit.

Other PCAP practitioners will work in private practice or for private clinics and will charge for their services. They are, of course, at liberty to do so. This is how they make their living and recoup the costs of the training, continuing professional development, professional registrations, insurance and supervision that maintain the high standards of their practice.

The hope behind this book and the UK-based charity which published it is that parents and carers can also be helped on the basis of need rather than their ability to pay. Living near Nottingham, I rather like to reference Robin Hood, who was known for helping the poor through his gain from the wealthy. Paid-for services are essential in this case because a proportion of these funds can enable pro bono services to be offered to other families who cannot pay.

Who can deliver Parent-Child Attachment Play?

This method is designed to be used by a wide range of skilled practitioners working with families. It is particularly aimed at those who can offer PCAP as an early help or pathway approach. It is likely to appeal to social workers, family outreach and support workers, fostering and adoption agency workers, psychologists, play and creative arts therapists, portage workers, early years specialists, teaching staff, and other suitably skilled and experienced professionals. PCAP practitioners need to be trained and licensed in the method and to update their knowledge regularly through continuing professional development activities.

What skills do Parent-Child Attachment Play practitioners need?

There is considerable skill involved in the effective delivery of PCAP; the simplicity of the approach does not equate to it being easy. In essence, PCAP practitioners need to embody the three skills being shared with parents and carers – play, containment and Reflective Functioning – detailed in full earlier.

Thus, PCAP practitioners need to be warm and playful and take their lead from the parent/carer. They need to be appropriately contained throughout the process, both internally and externally, with the parent/carer. For example, practitioners recognise the importance of providing a contained space in which to meet. They uphold professional boundaries with the parent/carer whilst being warm, sensitive and emotionally available to them. They are also gentle and clear about the PCAP process, including the expectation that the parent/carer will carry out the work as agreed. The PCAP practitioner also needs to reflect on her own thoughts, feelings and PCAP practice and ensure safe and effective working practices.

The practitioner needs to be highly adept at using Reflective Functioning skills, which hold the key to operationalising an attachment response:

- Head: holding the parent/carer in mind and imagining how things are for her
- Heart: tuning in to the feelings of the parent/carer and realising that her own feelings are separate from these whilst being in interplay with them
- Hands: being able to do or say something that enables the parent/carer to feel understood.

These RF skills need to be present both verbally and non-verbally, as we saw earlier.

What training and support do Parent-Child Attachment Play practitioners need?

PCAP practitioners must be trained in the approach. Whilst this book provides comprehensive theory, knowledge and guidance, it cannot reliably replace high-quality and accredited training. Face-to-face training is available in the UK and at a growing number of venues around the globe. Online training is also available if face-to-face training is not practical or available. An affordable and comprehensive two-day training course is offered, together with accredited certification. In addition, practitioners receive access to online resources including essential reading, academic papers, resources and paperwork, and a host of other creative PCAP ideas. Following the successful completion of training, practitioners can apply for a licence to practice PCAP which includes a commitment to quality assurance and ethical practice. This low-cost licence is renewable biannually and raises funds to maintain the online resource bank, implement quality assurance measures and continue the development of the method in line with newly-published empirical evidence and policy guidance.

Newly-accredited PCAP practitioners also have a mentor to support them during their early delivery. A total of three sessions are recommended: before setting the PCAP work up, midway through delivery, and reflection following the PCAP process. Mentoring can be provided as part of the training package and trainers can help PCAP practitioners find a mentor. Mentoring can also be provided through existing channels, for example through social work supervision. However, the mentoring must be process-driven and highly reflective rather than focused on case management.

Reflective practice is mandatory and PCAP practitioners complete a short sheet following each session which asks a series of questions designed to help them reflect on a number of key points and guide the work moving forwards. This reflective practice sheet can be found in the online resource bank. It also helps practitioners to identify child protection or other concerns, either for monitoring or referral.

What ethical framework do Parent-Child Attachment Play practitioners adopt?

PCAP practitioners operate within an ethical framework that guides their practice and policies on all levels. This framework consists of four principles: respect, competence, responsibility and integrity.

1. Respect: PCAP practitioners believe in the dignity and worth of all people regardless of difference, and are careful to uphold the individual rights of all those they work with. This includes parents, carers, children, other professionals, third parties and practitioners themselves. Self-respect and self-care are critical to the effective implementation of this method.

2. Competence: PCAP practitioners work within the limits of their knowledge, skill, training, education and experience. When needed, they refer to other professionals for guidance or refer parents/carers to specialist services. Reflective practice and professional mentoring are seen as essential to ensure competent working.

3. Responsibility: PCAP practitioners value their responsibilities to the families they work with, the general public and the reputation of PCAP, including the avoidance of harm and the prevention of misuse or abuse of their position.

4. Integrity: PCAP practitioners uphold honesty, accuracy, clarity and fairness in their interactions with families and all others during the course of their work.

In addition, PCAP practitioners must operate under a comprehensive set of legal guidance, insurance and policies which cover every aspect of their work with families. These may be provided by the umbrella organisation or agency under which the practitioner works, but individual PCAP practitioners are responsible for ensuring that they are in place before commencing PCAP work with families. These policies include, but are not limited to:

- child protection
- working with vulnerable adults
- lone-working

- home-visiting and safety (where practitioners work in parents/carers' homes)
- public liability insurance
- professional indemnity insurance
- risk assessment and reduction
- any country-specific legal requirements and/or government and procedural policy

What evaluation tools can I use to measure the outcomes of Parent-Child Attachment Play?

The robust and validated Tool for measuring Parental Self-Efficacy (TOPSE) is the recommended measure to use with PCAP (Kendall and Bloomfield, 2005). TOPSE is used in the UK and many other countries to evaluate a range of programmes to support parents and carers. It was developed in the UK in response to health professionals such as public health nurses and health visitors, who saw a need for a reliable and valid instrument with which to assess the outcomes of interventions with parents, carers and children. Following online registration, a free PDF of the tool, which comes as a parent-friendly booklet, can be downloaded from the TOPSE website (see below).

Parental self-efficacy can be defined as the belief and confidence that parents and carers have in their ability to carry out and manage the tasks of raising their child(ren) successfully. Hence, it is well-matched to the principles of PCAP as a method for empowering parents and carers as the change agents within their own family. Parental self-efficacy has been shown to be a critical factor in the quality of the parent-child relationship. Higher levels are associated with:

- increased quality of parent-child interactions
- increased parental warmth and responsiveness to children and teenagers
- parental involvement with and monitoring of teenagers.

In turn, these increases act as protective factors that reduce the likelihood of child and adolescent anxiety, depression and behavioural problems (Jones and Prinz, 2005). They are also associated with improved child and teen self-esteem, school performance and social functioning. Research has shown that parental self-efficacy can be changed through intervention programmes (ibid.).

TOPSE consists of 48 self-efficacy statements that address eight domains of parenting: emotion and affection, play and enjoyment, empathy and understanding, control, discipline and boundary setting, pressures of parenting, self-acceptance, and learning and knowledge. There are six self-efficacy statements for each domain and parents indicate how much they agree with each statement by responding to a Likert scale from 0 to 10, where 0 equates to complete disagreement and 10 equates to complete agreement.

Parents complete the TOPSE booklet during the second step of PCAP and this is repeated following the final step to determine any change in self-efficacy scores. Parents/carers are reassured that there are no right or wrong answers and that their scores are not being compared with others or with an "ideal" score.

Pre- and post-PCAP scores can be entered into a spreadsheet, and score changes overall and in the individual domains calculated and used for PCAP evaluation reporting.

Full details of the TOPSE measure, including its history and ongoing validation studies, can be found at www.topse.org.uk/site/

What resources do I need to deliver Parent-Child Attachment Play?

PCAP is relatively resource-light and much of the necessary kit can be sourced cheaply. The emphasis is on using everyday toys, creative materials, recycled materials and items found in many homes. The following list is indicative of what PCAP practitioners will need; all downloadable items can be found in the online resource bank.

1. PCAP infographic (Appendix 1), PCAP ten-step method summary document to guide the work (Appendix 2) and the PCAP programme planning sheet (Appendix 3)
2. Handouts for parents and carers on the three skills (Appendices 4b, 5b and 6b)

3. Practitioner's own example mini-kit to show parents/carers and to use during practice sessions. It is also used as a basis for opening discussions about what the parent/carer's individual child might like in her box or bag. Practitioners adapt the contents of the example kit as appropriate for each case
4. A choice of mini-kit resources and shoeboxes/bags if needed by parents/carers
5. Paperwork (various forms as appropriate)
6. Felt pens or similar and paper
7. Creative ideas for playful games with parents/carers (for example, noughts and crosses, making finger prints with an ink pad and turning them into faces or animals, and other quick, low-risk ideas)
8. One or two ideas for a creative toy to make with parents/carers
9. Soothing music on a smartphone for relaxation exercises with parents/carers
10. Other supportive supplementary activities for parents/carers as required (Appendix 7)

Practitioners always have their example mini-kit available for use throughout the practice sessions with parents/carers. Although parents/carers will have made their own fairly early in the process, they often forget to bring their mini-kit with them each week for practice and this does not matter. In fact, parents/carers need to keep in mind that the mini-kit they have created is for the child and not for them. Children may choose to use the mini-kit in different ways to those envisaged by the parent/carer. It is useful if this can be acknowledged and discussed to prepare for and contain strong reactions in the parent/carer when the mini-kit is introduced at home.

How do I become a licensed Parent-Child Attachment Play practitioner?

Affordable and accredited PCAP training is offered in the UK and at a growing number of venues in other countries. Online training is also available where practitioners cannot access face-to-face training. PCAP training is only available to those professionals already skilled and experienced in relevant direct work with families.

Following training, PCAP practitioners can apply for a licence stamp which shows commissioners, parents and carers that they adhere to the ethical and practice guidelines of the organising body that created PCAP and is responsible for supporting a growing number of PCAP practitioners. This support includes initial and top-up training, resources, quality assurance and evaluation tools. The organising body is big toes little toes, a UK-based charity, and details of licensing arrangements and all practitioner resources can be found at www.bigtoeslittletoes.org

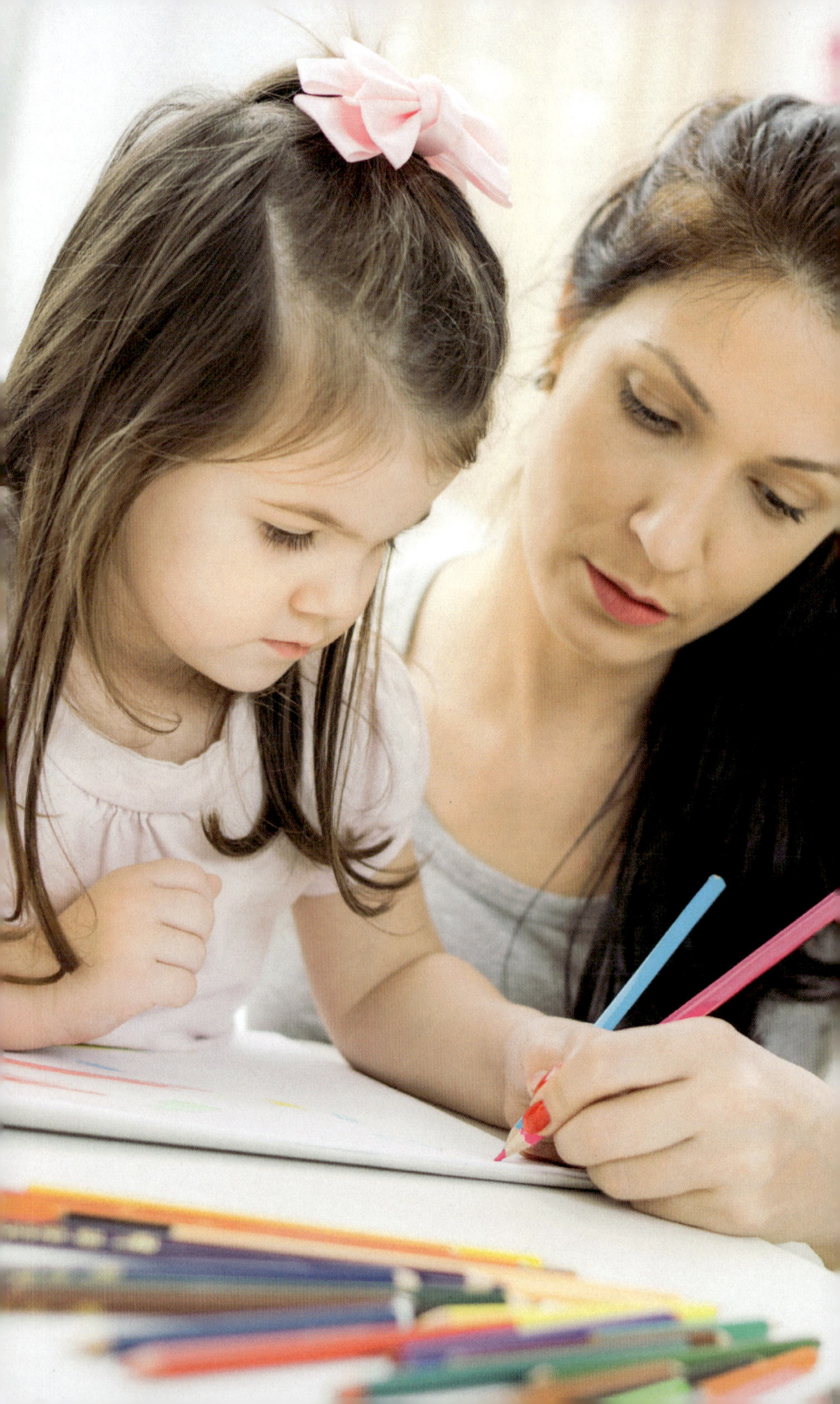

Part 2: The 10-step method

The ten-step method allows flexibility over the length of the process. The steps take place in the order given below but can take different formats and durations. Figure 2.1 represents an example timeline of PCAP steps. This is for a one-to-one format over a period of 12 weeks in total.

After the initial set of home-based playtimes, parents/carers are encouraged to continue in the same way, at least in the short term. In the longer term, they are encouraged to continue having a weekly one-to-one time with the child. This will change as time goes on; for example, the mini-kit might give way to another activity that the child enjoys.

WEEK	1	2	3	4	5	6	7	8	9	10	11	12
STEP	1 2	3	4	5	6 7	8			9			10
Meeting	✓	✓	✓	✓	✓	✓	✓	✓				✓
Home playtime					✓	✓	✓	✓	✓	✓	✓	✓
Phone email or text									✓	✓	✓	
Ending												✓

Figure 2.1: Example PCAP timeline by step and by week

Step 1: Building a relationship with parents and carers

The success of PCAP rests almost entirely on the quality of the relationship developed between parent/carer and practitioner. In turn, this relationship becomes the context in which the parent-child relationship is strengthened. Consequently, PCAP practitioners create a unique space in which the relational needs of the parent/carer can be met. The PCAP practitioner has two tools for use to develop the kind of working relationship that both maintains professional boundaries and meets the very human need for parents/carers to feel connected with the practitioner. PCAP may be a professional service to the practitioner and those who commission it, but to the parent/carer it is a trusting relationship dealing with intimate and difficult issues within her family life. The two tools are the PCAP principles and the practitioner's own RF capacity and use.

When meeting parents/carers for the first time, PCAP practitioners are guided by a set of principles which express the beliefs that underpin the PCAP method:

- parents/carers are best supported through a strengths-based method
- parents/carers must be empowered as change agents in their own families wherever possible
- families are best helped via an "inside-out" method, powered by growing internal motivation and relationship quality rather than behaviour modification
- RF is the overarching attachment-generative mechanism to both bridge any relational gaps in the parental history and to use in the ongoing relationship between parent/carer and child
- interactions between PCAP practitioner and parent/carer are playful and supportive and begin with RF and gentle, open questions

The above principles help the PCAP practitioner to adopt a reflective and intentional stance with parents/carers, which in turn allows a trusting and secure relationship to develop between them.

Parents/carers may come to the PCAP practitioner either through a referral process or self-referral. First impressions are extremely powerful and PCAP practitioners set up their first meeting carefully. Instead of focusing on any paperwork needed, it is better to focus on meeting the person herself and listening to the story she has to tell. Greeting parents/carers at the door, and leading them through to where they need to be, helps reduce anxiety. Placing a "Do not disturb" sign on the door helps them to feel that their time and privacy is being respected and valued. Inviting them to sit down and offering a glass of water or a hot drink will help parents/carers to relax and feel valued and important.

My experience tells me that most parents and carers are extremely anxious about PCAP, even if they consider their problems to be minor. They may worry about what the practitioner will think of them as a parent/carer; they may be concerned that sharing detailed information about their home life may land them in trouble; they may feel embarrassed; there are many understandable reasons why parents/carers may avoid seeking help or find it very difficult to begin the process.

My tried and tested way of validating many parental fears – without giving the impression that these may be fears held by the parent/carer in front of me – is to use the phrase "Many parents and carers want to know …".

Before we go on to illustrate how this might look in practice, I'd like to introduce a parent-child pair whose story will help to show the various PCAP steps in detail.

Karen is the 32-year-old mum of two children, aged three and five. Her five-year-old son, Daniel, is having real trouble at school and at home. The school has excluded Daniel a few times for outbursts and tantrums, and mum finds him very hard to manage at home. Hyperactivity has been mentioned, but mum is finding it very difficult to get a referral either to a pediatrician or to the local Child and Adolescent Mental Health Service (CAMHS) team for assessment. Mum is keen to get help and she is also worried about her daughter, Freya, who is showing signs of anxiety and stress. The school has commissioned me to offer PCAP to the family in a bid to intervene and support the mother before things begin to deteriorate further. Everyone is extremely concerned that Daniel is at risk of permanent exclusion from school at the age of five.

Please note that, whilst this case draws on many real PCAP families, it is fictitious in order to provide complete anonymity.

(Debi meets Karen at the school reception desk. They have already spoken on the phone a couple of times for Debi to introduce herself and the PCAP support on offer, and to set up the first meeting.)

Debi: *Hi Karen, I'm Debi* [shake hands]. *Nice to meet you in person!*

Karen: *Nice to meet you – it's pouring out there.*

Debi: *Typical! We're through here ...* (They walk along a corridor to a room – both walk in – Debi turns "Do not disturb sign" round. Debi smiles warmly at Karen.) *Can I get you a hot drink?*

Karen: *Tea would be nice, thanks, milk and one sugar.*

(Debi flicks kettle on and makes the drinks)

Debi: *Well, thank you so much for coming. It's very nice to meet you properly. I realise that we are here because things are very tough with Daniel.*

Karen: *You could say that.*

(Debi places drinks on table and is careful to sit alongside Karen, not directly opposite her)

Debi: *Today is a chance for us to get to know each other, decide if we think it's worth trying this method and to make a plan. Does that sound OK to you?*

Karen: *Yes, that's fine.*

Debi: *Also, many parents want to know about a number of things when we first meet: what is this person going to be like?; is she going to have the answers I need?; will she judge me or think I'm a bad parent?; will this method actually work, because nothing else has much?; what will I have to do?, etc.*

Karen (laughs): *Yep – all those and some other ones.*

Debi (smiling): *Do you want to add yours?*

Karen: *School makes me feel like a bad parent because Daniel kicks off and has to come home a lot. I feel like a naughty kid myself half the time when I'm here.*

Debi: *Hmm, like you're a problem too ...*

Karen: *Yeah, but I don't mind this room because it's tucked away. Is school going to find out what we talk about in here?*

Debi: *Good question. What we discuss in here is completely confidential and won't be shared with anyone else. The only exception to this would be if you told me that you or the children were at risk of harm and then I would have to pass this information on to the relevant person. I have a sheet detailing all of this which I can give you. I will write a brief report at the end of our work which I will share with you before finalising. School will also get a copy. This will only contain a brief and limited overview of our work together. It will also contain recommendations which we can agree if there are other things we feel can help after this.*

Karen: *OK – that sounds OK.*

Debi: *You can let me know at the end of today if you feel that we can work together well – that's important. I am not sure I have the answers you might be looking for, but I have some things we can try and see. The approach we can try is research-based so I am hopeful that it might help. I actually think that you have many of the answers yourself – we can see how we go.*

Karen: *Sounds good, but how long will it take?*

Debi (smiling): *I am guessing you want it to be as quick as possible, right?*

Karen: *That would be a relief, yes.*

Debi: *Well, we have six meetings together until half term and then another six next term.*

Karen: *OK.*

Debi (smiling): *Can you tell me about Daniel? Can you start from the beginning and tell me a bit about your pregnancy, his birth, his first year and how things have gone from there? I'm really interested to hear everything from your point of view …*

The PCAP practitioner is first interested in hearing the "story" of what has been happening and what parents/carers think has been going wrong. Any completion of family information or referral forms can wait until the parent/carer has told her story and had her worries, concerns and frustrations validated by the PCAP practitioner.

During the telling of the story, the PCAP practitioner listens carefully and accepts everything that the parent/carer shares without judgement. The occasional nod and non-verbal or short verbal reflection helps the parent/carer to continue her story knowing that she is heard.

Karen: *Actually, I think it might have something to do with when he was born, because he was premature and had to go in the special care baby unit. He was tiny and I remember being so scared that he wouldn't make it. I visited him twice a day when I was discharged from hospital. I remember feeling really* numb. But he did OK and came home after a month. He was a happy baby and seemed to be doing fine until he went to nursery. He was so clingy. They had to peel him off me. He didn't settle and had temper tantrums, threw toys around and hit other children. It just got worse when he went up to reception class. He has a really nice teacher, who helps him calm down most of the time. I am worried that he might have to go to a special school and I just want him to be happy, behave himself and learn like all the other kids.

Debi: *Thanks, Karen – that's really helpful for me to know. Sounds really, really tough. You're worried about what's going to happen to Daniel going forward.*

Karen: *I am very worried.*

Debi: *Can you tell me a bit about how Daniel feels about what's happening at school and home with his behaviour?*

Karen: *Well, he's happy when it's quiet. I think school's too loud and noisy for him sometimes. He likes his own space and to do things on his own terms. He's a bit stubborn, I guess. I worry that he hates school and doesn't want to go. I see him twiddling his hands in the car on the way and he makes me feel really anxious about dropping him off. Like something bad is going to happen.*

During the telling of the story from both perspectives, the practitioner listens carefully for any evidence of RF capacity shown in the parental narrative. She listens for evidence of mum using her

- Head - to hold Daniel in mind and think about what might be going on for him and from his point of view
- Heart – to tune into Daniel's feelings and to feel them and to know that they are separate from her own
- Hands – to let Daniel know through words or actions that she "gets" him, and that she is trying very hard to understand him and what is going on for him.

In Karen's story, there is some evidence of parental RF capacity but it is not extensive. Re-read the story so far and look for evidence of her use of Head, Heart and Hands. It is clear that Karen has the capacity to develop her RF further through PCAP. A copy of Karen's story, annotated for RF capacity, can be found in Appendix 8.

Next, the PCAP practitioner shares the parent-friendly version of

The 10-step Method

the PCAP method infographic (see Appendix 1) and leaves this with the parent/carer to keep. The practitioner explains the principles of PCAP, the three skills and the ten steps. The parent/carer is encouraged to ask questions or make comments as this goes along. At the end, the PCAP practitioner checks that the parent/carer understands that after a few weeks – and when she is ready - she will need to set up a home-based playtime for her child. She needs to be prepared to keep this time going for about six to eight weeks. It is best to get the parent/carer to agree to this at the beginning to avoid any difficulties later in the process. The parent/carer must be committed to offering the home-based playtime every week for the agreed period, even if the sessions do not appear to be going well.

At the end of the first meeting, the PCAP practitioner collects the relevant family, personal and contact details from the parent/carer. The two parties co-create a list of appointments and keep the same day, time and room venue throughout. They may use the PCAP planning sheet in Appendix 3.

The PCAP practitioner may end by asking the parent/carer to do some enjoyable "homework". I often begin with asking parents/carers to take five to ten minutes that afternoon or evening to do something that helps them feel relaxed and refreshed. This means different things to different people; for one it may be a bubble bath, for another a nice sit down with a coffee, for another a walk around the block. Find out the best idea from the parent/carer using open questions, and then let her know, with a smile, that you will check that she did her homework when you meet the following week.

Step 2: Assessing need, setting goals and optional parent-child play observation

In terms of assessing family needs, the PCAP practitioner has already heard the parent/carer's story about the child and her ideas about what the problem might be. The practitioner has listened out for the potential to develop RF in the parent/carer. In addition, the practitioner has two other ways to assess need: the TOPSE booklet and an optional parent-child play observation.

The PCAP practitioner can explain the TOPSE booklet to the parent/carer and either give her time to complete it or assist, question-by-question. Practitioners are very careful to emphasise that the parent/carer's parenting skills are not being assessed through this measure. Neither is her score being compared to other parental scores or to some kind of ideal. TOPSE is actually about measuring how individual parents and carers *feel* about being a parent and the many tasks this involves.

Sometimes it is useful for practitioners to see the parent/carer and child together, but this is not essential. This optional observation involves the parent/carer and child being asked to play together for ten minutes as they would normally do at home. The practitioner watches very carefully without comment or intervention. Discussion afterwards with the parent/carer is possible, but only if the child is not present. For example, if the observation takes place at school, it is relatively easy for the child to return to class. This is less easy in another setting. It is essential that no conversation takes place "over the child's head", which could be negative or unhelpful. If the play observation is happening in a setting outside school, it will need to be a separate meeting with no other assessment or discussion.

Let's return to Karen and Daniel and see how the play observation might look in practice. They have both arrived in the meeting room, and I have placed my PCAP mini-kit bag on the table and spread out a few toys.

Debi: *Hi Daniel, hi Karen. Great to see you both. Please come on in.* (Turns to Daniel). *Thank you so much, Daniel, for popping out of lessons today. I'm Debi, and your mum and I are learning some play ideas together in school. In a few weeks, Mummy will show you at home. I thought it would be really helpful to meet you and see you and Mummy playing together for a little while today.* (Daniel is already moving towards the table and toys. Karen looks a little uncomfortable and I give her a smile). *You want to play?* (To Daniel, smiling.) *How about you and Mummy have some time to look in the bag of toys and play together for about ten minutes. I'll sit over here and you can just ignore me! I'll let you know when there are five minutes left, then one minute, and when it's time to stop. OK, Daniel? OK, Karen? Just do what you normally do, there's no right and wrong with this.*

Karen: *Come on then, let's take a look!*

(Karen and Daniel look in the bag and take some of the toys out. Debi has put things in there which she hopes will interest Daniel. There are action figures of knights, dragons, wizards and fairies; and crayons and a pad of coloured paper. Wooden blocks of different shapes and sizes and an animal set complete the mini-kit. Daniel dives straight in and grabs two of the dragons.)

Daniel: *Good against evil!* (He smashes them together.)

Karen: *Who's gonna win?*

Daniel: *I don't know yet, the battle is very hard.* (He points to the wooden blocks.) *Mummy, build a castle.*

Karen: *OK.* (She builds the blocks up but then, without warning, Daniel knocks them down with a swoop of the dragons.)

Karen: *That's not nice, Daniel. Play nicely …*

The playtime continues and I let them know when there are five minutes to go and then one minute. After ten minutes, the playtime comes to an end and I thank both of them. Daniel is quite happy to return to his classroom and his mum tells him she will see him later. I am careful to avoid making any value statements about the playtime. Karen may want to ask about it and I can let her know that it was very useful to meet Daniel and get a feel for how they already play together.

The meeting may continue with the introduction of the three skills to Karen. If the parent-child observation is taking place in school, Step 2 and Step 3 are easily combined into one meeting. If not, it may be less easy to continue the meeting without the child also being in the room. When Karen has gone, I spend a few minutes reflecting on the playtime and complete the PCAP Play Observation sheet, which can be found in the online resource bank. This is designed to help me reflect on the starting point for Karen in relation to the three PCAP skills.

Step 3: Play (Skill 1)

The first skill to introduce to Karen is the play skill. In principle, Karen considers herself to be quite a playful person. However, we saw a little hint at the end of the play observation that she might have ideas about how Daniel should play "properly". I introduce the play skill using the handouts to guide me (see Appendices 4a and 4b).

As I talk with her a little about play in general, I learn that she enjoys playing games that have educational content and/or rules. She likes to be in control of the play. She also likes Daniel to follow the rules, and play in acceptable ways.

In this case, my aim is to accept Karen's preferences and gently explore with her a play approach that is more centred on Daniel and his preferences. I ask Karen about his favourite games and how he likes to play on his own and with his sister. Gently, Karen comes to realise that Daniel likes making things and playing with them. He has a great imagination and especially likes games of battles, which he generally wins.

Karen is open to the idea of facilitating "Daniel-oriented" play. I also sit alongside Karen and offer her the chance to enjoy making a simple toy. She has chosen to make a "treasure chest", sticking sequins and craft jewels onto a box. As we create this, Karen talks about things she used to play with when she was a child. Part of the discussion touches on the lack of playful interaction between her and her parents. I use my own RF to hold Karen in mind, to connect as best I can with her feelings, and to let her know that I am trying very hard to understand her experiences and feelings. I find that short statements like "That sounds tough" or "No wonder you felt that way" are helpful. Practitioners need to avoid three classic errors: making overly long reflections, repeating verbatim what parents/carers tell them, and using a questioning frame, for example "I'm wondering if you are feeling that maybe …"

I then show Karen my PCAP kit, which I have already adapted a little to Daniel's preferences. I have a bag filled with plastic soldiers and weapons, a few monsters and dinosaurs, bricks for building, recycled boxes and card, craft bits and bobs, safety scissors, tape and chunky crayons.

I begin the skill-sharing process and ask Karen to explore the things in the bag and to play as if she was a child for ten minutes. I'll let her know when we have five minutes left and then one minute, and then we can talk about how it felt to play.

Debi: *Here's the mini-kit.* (Puts it on the table.) *Please can you explore the toys in the bag and play a little as if you were a child. You are in charge of the play and I will follow your lead. You can invite me into the play, but you don't have to. I'll let you know when we have five minutes left and then one minute, and then we can chat about how it felt. There's no right or wrong here – just time to see how it feels to play.*

(Karen looks a little unsure, but picks up the bag and tips everything out. She gets the red-and-blue soldiers and starts lining them up.)

Karen: *Can you help me put these in a line?*

(Debi picks up the soldiers and follows Karen's lead, placing them in a long line. Karen gets a plastic monster and bashes the soldiers out of the way – they scatter and Karen laughs. Debi smiles. Karen repeats the process of lining the soldiers up and then bashing them down several times. Her mood then shifts and she changes to drawing a big blue shape on some card.)

Karen: *This is a lake – the lake of death.* (She is colouring it a dark blue.) *If you touch the water you die and sink into the depths.* (Debi is watching carefully. Karen takes a long time to create the lake and adds some trees around its edge.)

Debi (quietly): *We have five more minutes to play.*

Karen: *I just want to get this all finished, ready for the battle of the monsters against the soldiers.* (She finishes off. She appears to be setting the scene for a grand battle and uses all of the toys to build everything ready for it.)

Debi (quietly): *One more minute.*

(Karen sits back and looks at the scene. She looks up.)

Karen: *The battle is set.*

(Debi nods in agreement.)

Debi: *OK, our time is up ...* (Looks at Karen.) *How did that feel?*

Karen: *A bit weird to start with, but I got into it and actually quite enjoyed it. We don't really play much, do we? As adults, I mean ...*

Debi: *No, it's a while since we were kids – longer for me, though!* (The conversation continues, with Debi using her RF skills with Karen). *Now, can you have a try at giving me this kind of playtime? I'm going to explore the toys and play a bit. Can you let me take the lead and join in if I ask* you? You don't have to do or say anything, just let me play and help if needed. Ready? I'll let you know when we have five minutes and one minute left.

Karen: OK.

(Debi picks up the bag and empties the toys out. She starts sorting out the building bricks and asks Karen to count out ten for her. Karen does as she is asked).

Karen: *I am supposed to do that, aren't I – help, I mean?*

Debi: *Yes – I asked you to help me and you did – it was great.* (Debi continues to play and then gives Karen the five/one minute warnings.) *How did you find that?*

Karen: *It was alright now I'm getting used to this a bit.*

Debi: *Speaking as a child, I loved you playing with me. I felt important, and I liked how you responded to me and helped if I needed it. I liked how you didn't take over and you let me take the lead. I especially liked you spending time with me.*

Karen: *I didn't do very much – normally I'd be in there, doing stuff.*

Debi: *Was it OK sitting there, ready if needed?*

Karen: *I think so – it's just a bit different and I feel a bit awkward.*

Debi: *Like you should jump in and start playing too?*

Karen: *Yes, that's what I normally do.*

Debi: *This is just a different way of playing where we let Daniel take the lead.*

Karen (looking a bit fed up): *But he gets his way all the time – that's half the problem.*

Debi: *And this seems to just allow him to do that even more?*

Karen: *Exactly.*

Debi: *Next week we are going to look at the containment skill. Daniel can't just do what he wants – there are choices for him to make, and predictable consequences. This process takes a little while to bring everything in. We do a step at a time.*

Karen: *I'm glad there are rules …*

Please note that in PCAP we do not try to interpret the play content or create hypotheses about what it might mean. However interesting/pleasant/gentle/violent/gory the play is, we just accept and trust it.

The final part of the play skill is to support Karen to make a mini-kit for Daniel. We focus on things he enjoys and Karen is happy to source these for him. She remembers that she has a large plastic gift bag with Daniel's favourite superhero on it and decides to use this.

Step 4: Containment (Skill 2)

The process is now well underway and, when the parent/carer is ready, the process moves on to introduce the containment skill (see Appendices 5a and 5b). As with the other skills, this begins with an introduction and close attention to the parent/carer's thoughts and feelings about using it. As we have seen, Karen is keen on the idea of containing Daniel's behaviour during the playtimes. She feels that he gets his own way a great deal because of his behaviour and this understandably makes her feel angry and helpless.

I explain that containment in PCAP means making children feel safe and contained through words, actions or touch, or through managing time, space and the wider environment. I also explain that we use the containment ideas in various ways in PCAP.

I pick up the mini-kit and put it on the table. I explain that there are four rules for playtime: we look after you, we look after me, we look after the toys, and we stay in the space. Karen asks if she can add other rules if needed. I use my RF and reflect that these four rules do not seem strong enough for Daniel. Karen agrees. I then suggest that these rules could actually cover all kinds of things that might be relevant to Daniel. For example, Karen is worried that he will throw toys at her – this happens a great deal at home already. I reflect that the "look after me" rule can cover this. I listen to Karen's concerns, use my RF and let Karen know that I understand her worries given Daniel's extreme behaviour. We also sit alongside each other and make a poster of the rules and add pictures, a little like road signs. We laminate this and Karen is keen to put it in the mini-kit along with the toys. By now, she says that she is happy that having a few rules covering lots of different things makes it easier to remember them.

We then move to practising how to set up the playtime rules.

Debi: *This is how we might set up the playtime. I'll go first and then we can chat about it.* OK, so please imagine that you are a child and I am setting the playtime up for us. *OK, Karen, it's time for our playtime – 30 minutes, no more, no less – and here are the toys. We have four rules to keep: we look after you, we look after me, we look after the toys, and we stay in the space. OK? I'll let you know when we have five minutes and one minute left.*

Karen: *OK.*

Debi: *How did it feel when I set the playtime up like that?*

Karen: *Well, it is nice and clear, I suppose … but I still think Daniel will ruin our playtime, he usually does.*

Debi: *It's hard to imagine him being well behaved.*

Karen (looks tearful): *I want things to change but I have tried so many things before.*

Debi: *And you're afraid that PCAP will just be one more thing that fails to make a difference.*

Karen: *Yes … I want it to work but it seems a bit …* (Pauses.)

Debi: *Pathetic? How can playing for 30 minutes a week help?*

Karen (smiles): *Sorry, I didn't mean …*

Debi (smiles back): *It's OK, I don't mind at all. It's very normal to doubt this whole thing. We are going at your pace and we can try it and see. We have the research on our side, but sometimes it hurts too much to hope that things can change.*

Karen (looks relieved that Debi has voiced her fears and doesn't seem to mind at all): *I'll give it a go.*

Karen has a turn at introducing the playtime rules and uses the poster to help her. She is also very keen to work out what happens if Daniel chooses to break the rules.

Debi: *Let's try it during a mock playtime. Can you be a child and pretend to pick up a toy to throw it at me.*

Karen: *OK.*

(They begin to play and Karen picks up a brick and aims it at Debi's head.)

Debi: *Hang on, remember our rules. We look after you, we look after me, we look after the toys, and we stay in the space. OK. Ready to play? You can choose to break the rules again – it's your choice. I will just remind us of our rules again. You can choose to break the rules a third time – it's up to you. All that will happen is that playtime comes to an end, the toys go away and we will play again, same time, same day next week. OK?*

Karen: *Oh, I'm starting to see how this might work.*

Debi: *How did you feel when I explained that to you as if you were a child in the playtime?*

Karen: *You were very calm, no shouting, no drama ... I am not sure I can keep my cool.*

Debi: *That's honest! It's not easy ... we get to practise it a lot! We aim to keep it completely calm and predictable – like we mean what we say and say what we mean, in a gentle and firm way. Over time, many children begin to feel safe and boundaried and their behaviour choices improve. Sometimes, they test the rules lots of times to make sure we mean it. The rules are very reasonable and fair and Daniel will already have agreed to them. We'll just have to see how it goes when the playtimes start at home.*

We continue our discussions and then Karen has a go at maintaining the rules. As we discuss how she feels about holding the boundaries, the conversation moves back to her own experiences as a child and how punitive her father was. I use my RF skills to express my best efforts to accept and understand Karen's thoughts, feelings and experiences.

To support the containment skill, I introduce some breathing techniques, which we practise together, and I send Karen home with more nice homework which she has chosen – some circular mandalas to colour in to give her some mindful rest and relaxation.

Step 5: Plan home-based playtimes and review skills 1 and 2

This step involves helping the parent/carer to plan the home-based "You and Me" playtimes with her child. Sometimes it is relatively easy to get things into place, while on other occasions considerable extra resources may be needed. Once a day and time have been suggested by the parent/carer, any other practical arrangements around this need to be considered. Where there are other children in the family, the practitioner may need to help the parent/carer think about how best to look after them during the time their sibling is playing. This also includes how the others may feel about their sibling getting some lovely time with the parent/carer, and not them.

It is useful if the other children can have an alternative activity, which helps them manage any difficult feelings around the playtimes. For example, they may already be busy at the chosen time at a club or activity. Or perhaps they can have a playdate with a friend whose parent is happy to help. Sometimes, extended family can help out. Other options include having the playtimes at the weekend when the partner or a family friend is more easily available to assist with the other child(ren). Occasionally, it may be necessary to offer childcare support or to provide for the other child(ren) to go to an afterschool club to support the home-based playtimes.

This step also allows for the parent/carer and practitioner to reflect on how the process is going and how they are feeling about future playtimes. Again, the practitioner uses her RF skills to support the parent/carer: Head – thinking about the parent/carer and imagining things from her point of view; Heart – tuning in to the parent/carer's feelings and being able to recognise that the practitioner's thoughts and feelings can be affected by the parent/carer's, and vice versa; and Hands – the practitioner letting the parent/carer know that she is understood, both verbally and non-verbally.

As mentioned earlier – and worth repeating here – there are three classic errors for practitioners to avoid: repeating verbatim what parents/carers say to them as if this repetition represents reflection; making overly long statements; and using a questioning reflection, for example "I am wondering if you are feeling …". Aim for short statements that capture the essense of what the parent/carer is thinking or feeling. For example, "You're worried Sian won't even play," not "I am wondering if you might be worried about Sian maybe not playing with you?" Short statements (guesses) are good and, even if you get it wrong, the parent/carer will generally just put you straight. For example, in response to the practitioner's statement above, the parent/carer might say: "Actually, I'm more worried about playing myself!"

In Karen and Daniel's case, a Saturday morning is agreed for the future playtimes. Daniel's sister, Freya, is going to play at her cousin's house. Her cousin is the same age and Karen's brother and his partner are more than happy to help out with this arrangement.

Step 6: Head, Heart and Hands (Reflective Functioning) (Skill 3)

RF has been in use implicitly throughout the PCAP process so far. However, this is the step where we share RF with parents/carers *explicitly*. As we bring it into their consciousness and help them develop it, they can choose to use it as a tool to help them with their child(ren). The scene has been set ready with the play/activity as the language of the playtime and containment as the safe and boundaried space in which it happens. It is now time to bring the attachment-generative mechanism into conscious action.

I introduce the Head, Heart and Hands card to Karen, explaining that researchers have only recently discovered this active "ingredient" in parent-child relationships. The concept is introduced and explained as Head, Heart and Hands (see Appendices 6a and 6b), but I also share its technical name: Reflective Functioning. Karen is interested, and discussion follows. Karen is particularly encouraged because she recognises that she can do this. However, she is worried that her own difficult responses to Daniel's behaviour will get in the way.

Debi: *You're worried you will get so angry with him that you won't be able to keep your temper.*

Karen: *He winds me up so much, Debi – honestly, sometimes I don't know what to do with myself, I'm so frustrated and ….* (She runs out of words as her feelings begin to rise.)

Debi: *He knows how to press buttons you didn't even know were there.*

Karen: *Yes, it's as if he's trying to break me.*

(The session continues with Debi making another cup of tea and using her RF skills throughout)

Karen is feeling better and has enjoyed some of the breathing exercises and other techniques to try when we feel our children's behaviour beginning to activate those very overwhelming and difficult feelings. I have also shared a safeguarding message that sometimes we can't cope and need to walk away and calm down – make a hot drink, phone a friend, or get some air. This message is shared as something that all parents/carers need to do because all families struggle with their children at times – there is just a lack of discussion or openess about it in society. This makes it very scary for parents/carers to ask for help or admit to anyone that they are struggling.

We then move on to begin to practise the Head, Heart and Hands skill together.

Debi: *I'd like to break Head, Heart and Hands down and try them out. First, I am setting us both a challenge! We have to sit here together for one minute and think about ... what's your favourite food, Karen?*

Karen: *Chocolate.*

Debi: *We have to think about chocolate and nothing else for a whole minute. If our minds wander off or we start planning something for later, we just bring ourselves back to thinking about chocolate. OK?*

Karen: *I want some chocolate already!*

(They laugh together and Debi comments that they should have chosen Brussels sprouts or something.)

Debi: *Ready, go ...*

(The minute seems to go on forever and they smile at each other a few times.)

Debi: *I found that hard... my mind wandered off lots of times and I had to concentrate really hard.*

Karen: *I thought it would be easy, but it wasn't.*

Debi: *That's the Head part – let's have a practice playtime with you being a child and playing. Instead of chocolate, I'm going to think about you and hold you in my mind and, whenever my thoughts wander off, I'm going to keep bringing them back to you. OK?*

(Karen puts the toys on the table and nods. She begins to play and Debi practises holding her in mind as best she can. Debi lets Karen know the five/one minute warnings and the play ends.)

Debi: *How was that?*

Karen: *I could feel you thinking about me – I knew that you weren't daydreaming. My turn ...*

We swap roles and practise. The discussion and reflections afterwards show how hard it is to actually hold anything in mind for long. I share the research which shows that RF only has be "adequate" or "good-enough" for it to help strengthen attachment security. Karen now practises holding me in mind while we play. The following discussion again allows me the opportunity to use my RF skills to help Karen reflect on RF itself.

The process can now move to the "Heart" part of RF.

Debi: *Now that we are really holding each other in mind, we are going to add the Heart part. As you play as a child again, I'm going to really think about you and focus on you. As you play, I am going to try to climb in your shoes and see and feel what you are feeling. If you seem excited, I am going to try to feel your excitement, and if you seem frustrated or worried, I am going to try to feel that too.*

(They play and Debi practises trying to attune to Karen's feelings.)

In the subsequent discussion, Karen is again concerned that Daniel's behaviour might make her angry. She is very sure that she will have no problem catching his anger. This is an ongoing theme in this case study – the fear of being overwhelmed by Daniel's bad behaviour – and I accept this fear and help to name Karen's fears about what she might do – my own RF skills are sufficient to help Karen with this. Please note that if I felt that this case went beyond RF and Karen needed her own counselling or other help, I would pause the PCAP and help signpost her to a suitably qualified practitioner. In this case, Karen's worries and fears were safely contained within this attachment framework.

Karen: *OK, I'll have a go at Heart.*

(They play with Debi as a child and Debi makes sure that she is nice and clear with feelings during the play to support Karen with the early development of this skill.)

Karen: *You didn't like it when you couldn't get the bricks to stand on top of each other. It's hard to tell whether you were upset or frustrated.*

Debi: *Guessing is good – just trying to tune into our children's feelings helps them to feel safe with us. When you are trying like you were, I feel important. I feel like you really care about me. So much of the time, I feel misunderstood and criticised, but for that time, I felt peaceful.* (Debi shares insights into how a child might feel.)

To end this meeting, I ask Karen if I can read a relaxation story to her with some music, to see if she enjoys it and finds it helpful. Karen is happy to try it and then goes home with the relaxation music on her phone. I encourage her to take time for herself so she can cope better with the challenges of being a mum.

Example relaxation scripts can be found in the online resource bank. Additional activities to support the development of each skill are provided in Appendix 7.

At the next meeting, Head and Heart are recapped and the final piece – Hands – is introduced to Karen. This is where everything comes together.

Debi: *Final thing to practise! Hands. So, if you play as a child and I am going to think about you and try to connect with your feelings. Like we did last time. I am going to use my words, actions or even body language to let you know that I understand – that I get it, that I get you.*

Karen: *OK ... You make a camp over here with these soldiers and I am going to make one at this end.*

Debi: *OK.* (Follows Karen's lead.)

Karen: *There is going to be a big battle, it's going to be a battle between good and evil.* (She shudders.)

(Debi tilts her head, catches Karen's eye and shows with her concerned expression that she understands that this battle is very frightening. She gently moves a little closer to Karen, looking ready for the battle – in her mind she thinks, *I am here with you.*)

Karen: *We need to call for help. I am going to write a letter and you will deliver it to the Kingdom over the hill. Strap it to this eagle. Hurry!*

(Debi follows the instructions quickly and carefully.)

Debi: *The message has gone.*

Karen (sighs heavily): *Good – we need more soldiers to come.* (Debi also sighs, and nods slowly.)

Debi: *You need a big army for this battle.*

Karen: *Yes.*

(The play continues.)

In the discussion, I ask Karen how she felt having me there thinking about her, tuning into her feelings and trying to let her know that I understood. She noticed that I didn't say much and that some of it happened non-verbally. She likes this because she says she might find it hard to know what to say.

Karen goes on to have a try at offering me a playtime with Head, Heart and Hands. During this playtime, I try hard to give obvious opportunities for Karen to practise. After the play and discussion, I share insight into how Head, Heart and Hands might make a child feel in operationalising a secure attachment response.

Debi: *Being with you makes me feel safe. As you let me know that I was understood, my body relaxed like a big breath out. It calmed me down because I knew you understood. I feel connected to you, I want to be with you, I know that you can cope even if I'm feeling bad. You feel strong and dependable.*

The Head, Heart and Hands skill is the most important skill, and parents/carers respond to it differently. With some, it is as if they have had some kind of epiphany – it makes perfect sense and they quickly get the hang of it. Others are anxious that they are not getting it right or not doing it enough. A few find it very hard and may even need a different way of beginning to explore these ideas. An alternative way of helping parents/carers with RF is to use the "Behaviour, Meaning, Feeling" approach first.

This technique is a guided observation using three prompts. The PCAP practitioner invites the parent/carer to play and, as she does so, she explains:

Behaviour: *I am going to really watch you and notice everything you do – your breathing, your movements, what you are doing and how you are playing.*

Meaning: *What does your behaviour mean? – What are you trying to tell me?*

Feeling: *What is the feeling behind this behaviour? –What feeling are you trying to communicate to me?*

Behaviour, Meaning, Feeling can be used to help parents/carers who may find the Head, Heart and Hands tool a little too conceptual to begin with. The advantage of starting with child behaviour is that it encourages parents/carers to really watch their child. From this careful observation, it is possible to help parents/carers begin to see that behaviour is the communication of thoughts, intentions and feelings. This is a more concrete way in for some parents/carers.

Step 7: Begin playtimes at home

The three skills are now coming together well and the parent/carer is ready to begin the weekly playtime at home with her child. Many parents/carers are able to introduce these without the practitioner present. Sometimes, the PCAP practitioner is there for the first couple of playtimes to ease the transition for the family. If this is the case, they say hello to the parent/carer and the child, and then sit in the corner of the room, out of the way. If this were the case with the home playtimes between Karen and Daniel, it might look like this:

(Debi arrives at Karen's house and smiles warmly at mum and son.)

Debi: *Hi! Great to see you both. Daniel, I enjoyed meeting you at school a few weeks back. Mummy and I have been learning some play ideas together. I'm here today to help you both get it started in your house.*

(They move to the front room, where the mini-kit is already on the big rug.)

Debi: *I'll just sit over here like I did before. I'm not in the playtime and won't be playing. It's just you and Mummy. OK? Mummy, are you OK to start the playtime off just like we practised?*

Karen (looks anxious): *Yes, I think so.*

Debi (smiles gently and warmly, acknowledging that Karen is worried): *I'm just over here.*

(Karen introduces the playtime and the four rules, and the playtime starts.)

Karen and Daniel enjoy their first playtime with the practitioner there simply as a containing and supportive presence. The usual difficulties in the parent-child relationship rarely come up in these supported playtimes but, if they do, I can offer Karen gentle support with the playtime rules. I can facilitate Karen but not take over her role. After the playtime, there may be a short opportunity to discuss it with Karen – if Daniel is happily engaged elsewhere in the house. If this is not possible, I contain Karen by letting her know that it was a great start. The next meeting between us is also confirmed and these continue until the home playtimes are well established.

Step 8: Transfer skills to problematic areas of home life

Once the three skills are developing nicely during the home-based playtimes and parents/carers are feeling more confident about implementing them, practitioners can begin Step 8. This step is absolutely essential to the successful transfer of skills into problematic areas of family life. It is the best opportunity that practitioners will get to help parents/carers work out how they can best transfer the skills. Let's catch up with Karen to see how this could look in practice.

(The session is already underway and Karen has explained that playtimes are still going well and that Daniel has really calmed down. He only broke the rules on one occasion, which was quite a surprise to Karen. She is now keen to see how the playtimes can help with other challenging times in daily family life.)

Karen: *Getting him out to school in the morning is still a real battle and we are late so often. I end up shouting, and the louder I get, the less he seems to care.*

Debi: *Stressful stuff.*

Karen: *Yes, so what can I do about it?*

Debi: *Let's have a think about the skills we have been using in the playtimes and how they might help. Any ideas?*

Karen: *Do you think it would help if I did the five-minute, one-minute thing in the morning?*

Debi: *Great idea, giving him a five-minute heads-up that it is nearly time to go and then a one-minute heads-up when you want to leave the house. This may well help him regulate better.*

Karen: *I could try letting him know that I understand that he finds the mornings hard and that I am here to help him.* (She laughs.) *I also think I need to do those relaxation exercises we did to keep my temper under control.*

Debi (smiling): *That's very honest! I think it's definitely worth trying your ideas. I'm also wondering about the way in which the playtime has such a predictable routine.*

Karen: *What, you mean like, here's the box, here's the space, this is what happens etc.?*

Debi: *Exactly. How could this help in the mornings?*

Karen: *Keeping it the same, maybe me helping a bit more with laying out his uniform, always doing things in the same order – that kind of thing.*

Debi: *I think that might really help. Tell you what, have a go and we can chat about it next time.*

The hope is that, over time, the various PCAP skills and supporting activities and strategies that practitioners may share with parents and carers belong to them. Practitioners are careful to sit back, use open questions and allow time for parents/carers to sometimes take a while to embrace new ways of thinking about their relationships with their children. Much better that parents/carers begin to come up with their own ideas of how they can try their growing skills outside the ring-fenced playtimes. We can tell parents/carers over and over how we feel they should behave, but this is highly unlikely to result in the "inside-out" change that PCAP embodies. Of course, some parents/carers find the transfer of skills to general family life much harder than others. The length of time needed for Step 8 will vary accordingly.

Step 9: Gently move to phone/text/ email support

Once home-based playtimes are established and consistently going well, the weekly face-to-face meeting between PCAP practitioner and parent/carer can shift to a weekly phone conversation, text or email. This can continue until the ending meeting, which is covered below. The parent/carer can continue the playtimes at home for around six to eight sessions. She can then continue for another block if desired or she can maintain the principle of having a weekly "You and Me" time with the child in a different form. This may change, especially as the child grows older, but the principle of having a one-to-one time together each week is encouraged to become part of family culture going forward.

A final ending meeting with the PCAP practitioner is in the diary and phone conversations, texts and emails keep the support going at a greater distance.

Step 10: Ending and reporting

This meeting brings the PCAP method to an end and can bring mixed feelings for both parent/carer and practitioner. Whilst parents/carers are enjoying feeling empowered within their homes, they may also be nervous about PCAP coming to an end. The containing and contained presence of the PCAP practitioner and her skilful use of RF has resulted in a secure relationship between her and the parent/carer. Even though the relationship has always been accepted as time-limited, it can be hard to say goodbye to each other. Preparing for the ending began when the practitioner first introduced the ten steps of PCAP. As each step has been completed, the practitioner has ensured that this is marked and acknowledged. The ending has been in sight for a while before it actually arrives.

It is ideal if the parent/carer can decide how she would like to end. The practitioner can then facilitate this. For many parents/carers and workshop groups, this involves sharing some favourite food and drink. For others, it involves a creative activity. Once, these ideas were even combined into the creative icing of homemade cupcakes and a pot of tea to share.

The final meeting also provides for evaluation, completion of the TOPSE booklet, discussion, and agreement around the final report. An example evaluation form can be found in the online resource bank. Care needs to be taken over literacy and language levels. The form is designed to capture the thoughts, feelings and views of the parent/carer – the qualitative data.

The TOPSE booklet is already familiar to parents/carers, having been completed at the beginning of the process. A comparison of the pre- and post-PCAP scores provides an overall score and individual scores across domains – the quantitative data.

If a final report is required, I share and discuss a draft with parents/carers. It has been carefully worded to reflect the strengths-based nature of the PCAP method. It may make recommendations, which should also be seen as supportive. It may have gaps, to be filled with the pre- and post-PCAP TOPSE scores once these have been calculated. A copy of the final report is usually sent to parents/carers, and to the body commissioning the work where relevant. An example (fictitious) PCAP report (for Karen and Daniel) is included in the online resource bank.

Finally, a PCAP certificate is given to the parent/carer (again, an example can be found in the online resource bank). This is designed to value, appreciate and mark the commitment and application given by the parent/carer to the PCAP process. Most parents/carers are really pleased to receive the certificate. In some cases, I have framed the certificate to lend more weight to the sense of achievement. For some parents/carers I have worked with, this is the only certificate they have ever received.

Sometimes, there is the option to offer the parent/carer a follow-up meeting or phone call after an agreed period of weeks and/or months has passed.

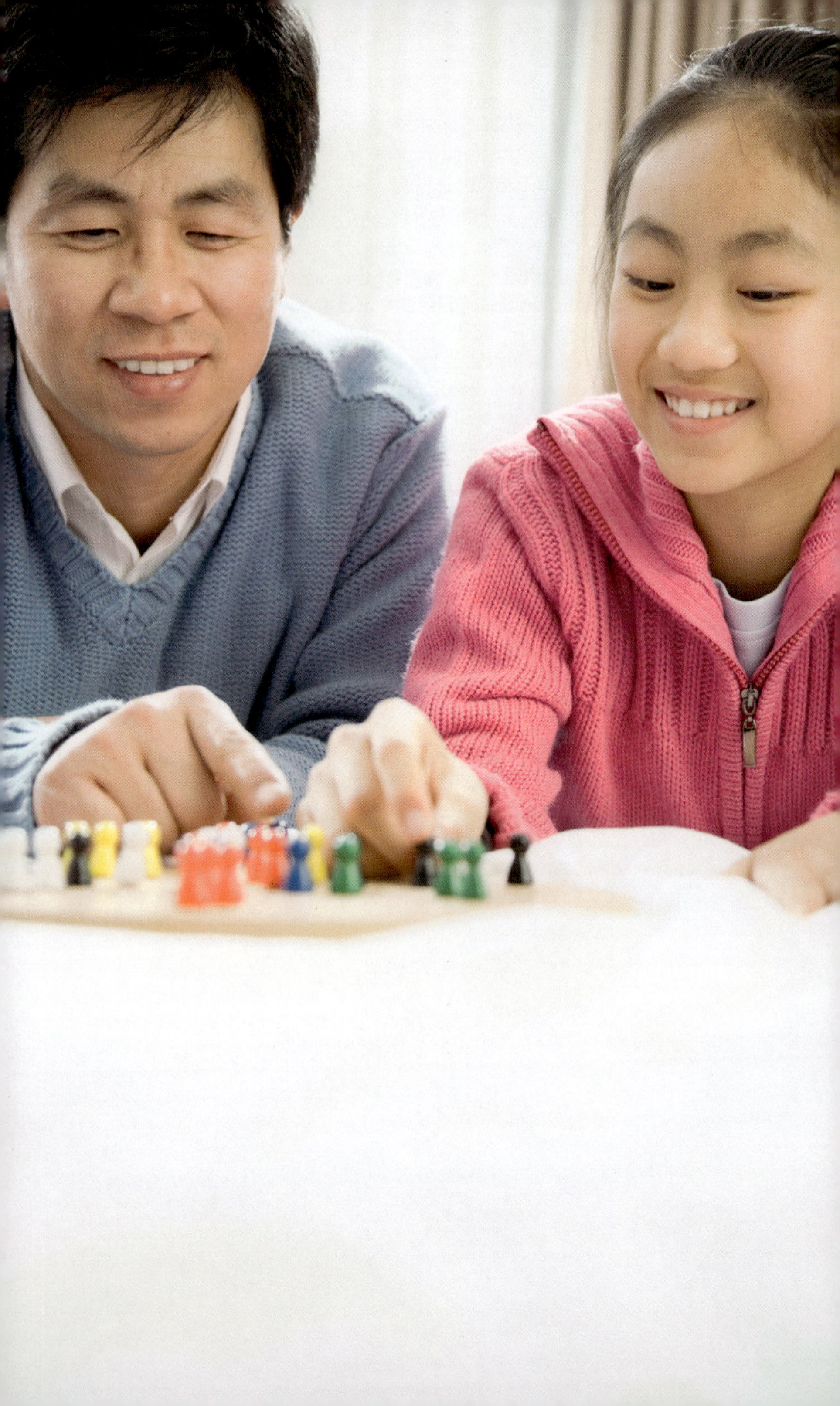

Part 3: The one-step or "light" version

There are some circumstances in which it is not possible or practical to offer the full ten-step PCAP method. Perhaps the practitioner is in the process of working directly with the child and meets the parent/carer just a few times to review the work. Perhaps the practitioner is actually delivering another type of help or support with the family and wants to "sprinkle" PCAP ideas onto this. Or perhaps the family situation between parent/carer and child is under great strain and the full PCAP method is not going to be either realistic or effective.

In such cases, practitioners can offer the one-step or "light" PCAP method. This involves asking parents/carers to think of an activity that their child really enjoys, and to provide this once a week. During this activity, the parent/carer is asked to practise Head, Heart and Hands. The activity may be a play or activity kit, or something else; for example, making breakfast together at the weekend, playing interactive computer games, playing cards or a board game, a craft kit, learning to swim together, or playing ball in the park. There are many possibilities.

A particular advantage of this approach is that the parent/carer can choose to practise her RF skills even without the child or teenager knowing. This is perfectly ethical and can avoid difficulties in the relationship. For example, a foster carer can be supported to choose times to practise RF through Head, Heart and Hands with their child or teen to ease the relationship and begin to strengthen attachment security. Bringing this to the child's attention might cause serious difficulty.

Other examples of where the one-step approach might be appropriate are:

- practising RF with a group of adopters who are awaiting a match – the full PCAP could be offered on placement
- supervising social workers sharing RF with foster carers as part of their ongoing training and support – again, full PCAP could be offered in some individual cases
- sharing RF with individual families who are receiving other support services, for example services for children with additional needs
- sharing RF as a technique for teachers and support staff to adopt in school
- equipping midday supervisors with RF skills to help create emotional safety in the playground
- health professionals sharing information about attachment and RF with pregnant mothers and partners
- childcare practitioners understanding how they could use RF in their setting to help very young children feel emotionally safe and secure

There are many possibilities, because RF is a powerful attachment mechanism and intervention in its own right. The advantage of the ten-step PCAP method is that it takes the parent/carer through a supportive process designed to embed RF directly into the family home. For many families, this is essential to bring about the kind of change that parents, carers, children and practitioners hope for.

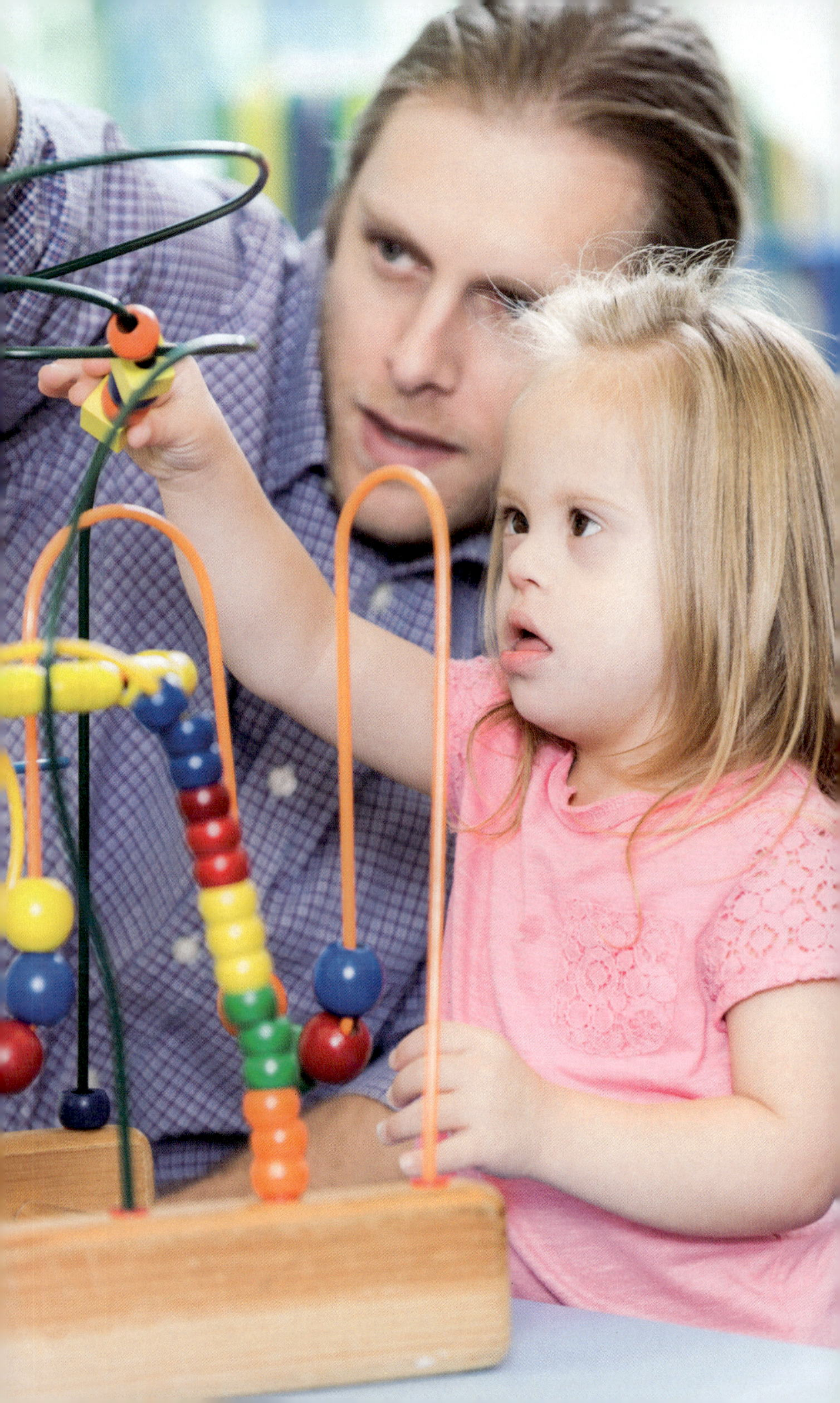

Conclusion

This book has outlined an innovative method to support parents and carers to become the change agents in their own families: Parent-Child Attachment Play. The principles in which the method is embedded have been presented along with the three skills shared with parents and carers. The ten-step method to empower parents/carers takes us from the very first meeting between practitioner and parent/carer right up until strengthened parent-child relations are being employed and enjoyed in the family home. The one-step or "light" version explains how to use a single attachment mechanism to empower parents, carers and even other practitioners. Finally, the book has provided considerable guidance and resources for those wishing to begin practising the approach.

The book began with a plea to move away from the concepts of "parenting" and "parenting styles", with the possible problems inherent in their use and relevance. Instead, this book calls for a strengths-based relational approach. First, the building of an authentic, reliable and trusting practitioner-parent relationship, which in turn sets the scene for the nurturance of the parent-child relationship. PCAP aims to be a respectful, no-blame, no-shame approach in which the practitioner walks alongside the parent/carer as she seeks to bring about the lasting difference she hopes for. Its practical and forward-facing focus enables the necessary work to come from a place of strength rather than criticism or weakness.

Lastly, children do not choose their early relationships, and by the time relationship difficulties are entrenched they are already interrupting and compromising the child's future outcomes. How much better to offer easily accessible support to families as a universal health promotion or early intervention strategy which heads off some of these difficulties before the damage begins to appear?

PCAP is unique in its active attachment mechanism and the particular way it delivers this into the family home via the parent/carer and practitioner relationship. As parents and carers practise the PCAP skills with their children within a supportive framework, the future really is looking brighter for the whole family.

Appendix 1

What is PCAP?

Handout for parents and carers

What is Parent-Child Attachment Play?

3 SKILLS:

- ✓ Play
- ✓ Containment
- ✓ Head, Heart, Hands

10 STEPS:

1. Parent/carer meets PCAP practitioner
2. Set goals
3. Play skill and prepare mini-playkit
4. Containment skill
5. Plan parent-child home playtimes
6. Head, Heart and Hands skill
7. "You and Me" playtime begins at home
8. Roll out playtime skills to everyday family life
9. Change to phone/text/mobile support
10. Ending

Empowering parents and carers as change agents in their own families

Appendix 2

**10-step method
Practitioner Summary**

10-step method summary

1. Introductions and hearing the parent/carer's story
2. Assessment, Parent-Child play observation (optional) and goal-setting
3. Skill 1: Play
    a. Learning how to play together/make own toy
    b. Play simple games with parent/carer to unlock playfulness
    c. Parent/carer plays as *a* child with practitioner – reflections led by question "How was that?"
    d. Practitioner plays as *a* child with parent/carer – follow with reflections from practitioner: "How was that?" and "I felt ......" (give the parent/carer positive insight into how the child might feel)
    e. Make a mini-kit for "You and Me" playtimes at home
4. Skill 2: Containment
    a. Introduce four playtime rules and make a poster
    b. Practitioner models setting up play session with the four rules – reflections as above
    c. Parent/carer practises setting up rules with practitioner – reflections and "I felt" insight
    d. Practitioner models how to hold the rules if the child tries to break them – reflections with parent/carer
    e. Parent/carer practises how to hold the rules if the child tries to break them – reflections and "I felt" insight
    f. Practitioner explains how to end the playtime (five minutes to go and one minute to go)
5. Plan home-based playtimes with parent/carer – revise skills 1 and 2 – repeat as needed
6. Skill 3: Head, Heart and Hands (RF)
    a. Practitioner models "Head" (really focusing on the child and keeping them in mind) during parent play – after practice, reflections as above

    b. Parent practices "Head" with practitioner playing as *a* child – reflections as above and insight from practitioner
    c. Repeat process with "Heart" and "Hands"
    d. Share "Head, Heart and Hands" card with parents/carers
7. Plan, set up and begin "You and Me" playtimes at home
8. Continue weekly sessions with practitioner until playtimes are going well at home. Discuss transfer of skills into problematic areas of home life; for example, using a "choice and consequence" to help children manage their behaviour, giving children a "five minutes/one minute to go" heads-up to help them prepare for something, making a poster of agreed positive rules for the whole family, etc.
9. Phone meetings/email for support
10. Ending and reporting

Tips on reflections

When parent/carer is experiencing each skill first – practitioner reflects with question "How was that?" or similar

When parent/carer practises each skill – practitioner reflects with question "How was that?" or similar

Then practitioner reflects with "I felt ..." e.g. "I felt special because you played with me", "I felt safe because I knew what the rules were and what would happen if I chose to break them" etc. This is to help parent/carer to gain insight into how a child might feel; to encourage parents to see things from the child's point of view; and to give the child a voice in the process

Parent/carers will also want to discuss how easy or hard they find each skill – practitioner validates and uses RF with parent/carer to create a safe and secure relationship with them.

Appendix 3

Our PCAP Programme Planner

Blank planning sheet for practitioners and parents/carers

Our PCAP Programme

Date and time	Meeting	Home-based playtime	Email, text or phone call
eg. 2 Feb 2017 10-11am	✓		

Appendix 4a

Practitioner guidance for
Play skill

Practitioner guidance
Skill 1: Play

1. Toys in the mini-kit are available to the child to use as she wishes (subject to the few agreed rules – see Skill 2: Containment)
2. Child leads, parent/carer follows the play where possible
3. Parent/carer does as the child directs (again, subject to the few rules)
4. Parent/carer takes on any role given by the child
5. Parent/carer positions herself next to or alongside the child, NOT directly opposite
6. The play happens in a contained space (see Skill 2).

Mini-kit

1. A bag or shoebox with a selection of toys chosen for the child by the parent/carer
2. These toys are not part of the child's usual toy collection
3. The parent/carer thinks about the child and the things she might like to play with. This is often a mixture of imaginative and creative toys; for example, cars, figures, paper and crayons, puppets, building blocks, soldiers, toy money, craft materials, glue stick, safety scissors, sellotape. However, children who play differently (for example, who prefer structured play and/or board games) can have these items in their mini-kit. Include safe items found around the house and free/recycled items to make the kit accessible for all families.

HINT: We suggest a limit of £5 to spend on the contents of the mini-kit. When working with families with no means, I provide a range of materials and the parent/carer chooses, say, 10–12 items that she thinks her child will like.

Appendix 4b

Parent/carer handout for Play skill

Skill 1: Play

Parent/carer provides a shoebox or bag of toys or suitable activities

Child leads the play and the parent/carer follows

Parent/carer does not tell the child what to do and joins in when asked

Parent/carer sits alongside the child during playtime

The playtime does have rules (covered in Skill 2)

THE MINI-KIT

A bag or shoebox with a small selection of toys or activities - chosen for the child by the parent/carer

Toys don't have to be new, but are not part of the child's usual toy collection

No more than £5!

Appendix 5a

Practitioner guidance for Containment skill

Appendix 5a

Practitioner guidance
Skill 2: Containment

1. The play takes place in a contained space, for example on a large rug in the living room or on the kitchen table. It is warm and quiet without disruption. Telephones/mobiles off
2. The parent/carer begins the playtime in the same way each week: "It's time for our playtime. We have 20 (or 30/40 minutes) no more, no less and there are just a few rules for us to keep"
3. Parent/carer reminds the child of the few rules each week: "We look after you, we look after me, we look after the toys, and we stay in the space"
4. Parent/carer reminds child that she can CHOOSE to break the rules – the first time you will remind her of the rules, the second time you will remind her that if she CHOOSES to break the rules once more then playtime will come to an end. That's OK – playtime will come again soon
5. Parent/carer MUST hold the rules and if the child chooses to break them for a third time the parent/carer simply acknowledges that the child has made a choice to end play. The parent/carer gathers up the toys and puts them away. The parent/carer might reflect that it is hard for the child to end. Playtime will carry on next week. The parent/carer remains calm, gentle and firm. No punishment is given. Withdrawing playtime is not allowed. If at all possible, the parent/carer stays with her child to help her with any overwhelming feelings around stopping. Sometimes it is helpful to move into the kitchen to get a drink
6. Parent/carer practises being "bigger and kinder" – in a way that makes the child feel very safe and secure
7. The parent/carer is completely calm and predictable before, during and after playtime

Appendix 5b

Parent/carer handout for Containment skill

Skill 2: Containment

This means helping the child to feel safe through the parent/carer's words, actions, choices, consequences and managing the environment

Playtime happens on the same day, at the same time, every week

Playtime happens in a contained space like on a large rug in the living room or at the kitchen table

It is warm and quiet – mobiles are off

Playtime starts the same every week: "It's time for our playtime! We have 20 (or 30/40) minutes, no more, no less, and there are just a few rules for us to keep".

Four rules for playtime: we look after you, we look after me, we look after the toys, and we stay in the space

Child can CHOOSE to break the rules – that's OK – the first time, remind her of the rules, the second time remind her that if she CHOOSES to break the rules a third time then playtime will come to an end. That's OK, playtime will come again soon

You MUST hold the rules even if this is hard! If your child chooses to break the rules for a third time, simply acknowledge that the child has made a choice to end. Gather up the toys gently and put them out the way. It's OK. Playtime will carry on next week. Remain calm, gentle and firm. No punishment is given

Withdrawing playtime is not allowed. If at all possible, stay with your child to help her if she is upset, frustrated or angry

Sometimes it is helpful to get a drink and change rooms

Practise being "bigger and kinder" so that your child feels very safe and secure

Be completely calm and predictable before, during and after playtime – taking time to breathe can help!

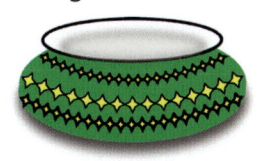

Appendix 6a

Practitioner guidance for Head, Heart and Hands (RF) skill

1. Head

During playtimes, think about your child. Put yourself in her shoes and see the world from her point of view. Give her your whole attention – actively think about her. Notice when other thoughts come into your mind, and let them go. Keep bringing your attention to the child. HOLD HER IN MIND. No need to say anything at this point – just really think and focus on your child

2. Heart

During playtimes, feel your child's feelings as much as you can. Watch her body language and facial expressions closely, sometimes using your own face to mirror them. Practise noticing her feelings affecting your feelings. Differentiate between which feelings are hers and which are yours. Notice the qualities of her play and what this means about her feelings – for example, bashing dinosaurs together aggressively may represent frustration or anger, or it might mean something completely different. No need to say anything at this point – see if you can feel your child's active and changing emotions

3. Hands

Do and say things that let your child know that you "get" her. Let her feel understood by nodding, mirroring facial expressions and using short statements. For example, your child is frustrated trying to do something and you say "so frustrating, eh?" Short statements are best, and guessing is good. She may ask for help, but do not help your child unless she indicates that this is wanted. She may seem happy about something, and you catch her eye and smile too. Guessing is fine – children really appreciate it when we are trying to understand them. It makes them feel safe and secure. They will put us straight if we get it wrong. HINT: Non-verbal reflection is as important as verbal!

Appendix 6b

Parent/carer handout for
Head, Heart and Hands (RF) skill

HEAD

Thinking about my child and wondering what she is thinking about. Focusing just on her. I wonder what is on your mind?

HEART

Putting myself in my child's shoes and imagining how she feels. Guessing is good. How are you feeling?

HANDS

Doing and saying things that let my child know that I am trying to understand her.

Appendix 7

Extra activities to support development of the three skills

Skill 1: Play (and mini-kit)

Learning to play – ask what things the parent/carer might like to play with and provide them

Start with a very simple game like noughts and crosses, or a culturally-appropriate game

My personal favourite – use a small colour ink pad and make fingerprints on paper with parent/carer – have fun adding pen strokes to turn them into funny faces or animals, insects, etc.

Ask parent/carer to remember something she used to play with as a child – see if you can source this or play something similar (avoid this if the parent/carer's own childhood history has been difficult)

For highly structured parents/carers, begin with a game with rules and then try more creative play

For parents/carers who seem to find containment challenging, start with free play and also try a structured game with rules to follow

Make a toy together – this is for the parent/carer, not the child – for example, using a bangle or wooden curtain ring with strips of ribbon, wool etc. tied on to make a streamer toy. I also make a glitter shaker with parents/carers – a recycled water bottle filled with water and glitter tipped in through a funnel and the lid taped on. I advise a very simple, cheap toy idea made from everyday items that are robust. We also use the bottle idea with parents/carers who have teenagers, and fill them with fun, unusual things like nails, paper clips or bolts (glue or tape the lid on carefully!)

Skill 2: Containment

Guided relaxation which helps parents/carers deal with difficult feelings aroused in them by their children

Affirmation cards – "I am a good-enough parent", "Keep calm, breathe and carry on"

Poems or song words to encourage parents/carers

Breathing exercises (see online resource bank)

Mindfulness colouring and other techniques

Developmental information about children and teens given in small, accessible "bite-sized" chunks – helps parent/carer to have a better understanding of her child and more realistic expectations of maturity and behaviour (ideas are regularly added to the online resource bank)

Five minutes for the parent/carer each day – looking after herself will help her contain her child(ren) – a walk, a coffee, a bubble bath, time to herself

Information on parent/carer telephone and Internet support services – for example, Family Lives, a UK-based confidential helpline for parents/carers

Skill 3: Head, Heart and Hands (RF)

Introduce the idea of holding her child in mind in a fun way – I ask parents/carers to think about bananas for a minute and to notice how many times their minds wander to other things. I also give parents/carers a picture of a banana to stick on the fridge at home as a fun way to remind them to hold their child in mind a little

Prepare some fun faces of children, teens and adults – play a guessing game – what are they thinking? Even add thought bubbles. I've even used animal faces – monkeys, dogs, raccoons, meerkats, etc. – to get this going in a non-threatening way

Ask parent/carer to think of an animal and you try to guess what she is thinking of – ask her to give you a bit of a clue – then guess – swap over

Same game but parent/carer thinks of a feeling – you try to guess what it is – ask her to give you a clue – swap

Invite the parent/carer to play a game with you – she is going to draw a shape that is easily recognisable – like a house, a flag or a teddy bear – anything that isn't too hard to draw! However, she can only do one stroke at a time. Say, for example, she draws a straight line and in her mind it's the wall of a house. I have to try to guess what she is drawing and add the next stroke (in a different colour). She can either use my stroke (if it's right) or maybe she has to ignore it and carry on with her idea – we see how long it takes for me to get in tune with what she is thinking

Collect some YouTube clips – I use funny clips of animals where things go wrong – we watch them and then pause to guess what is coming next – what is the main character thinking and feeling? We try to put words into the characters' mouths

Look out for creative ways to encourage parents/carers to watch and observe others and try to guess what they are thinking and feeling

Appendix 8

Karen's story annotated for evidence of parental Reflective Functioning capacity

Karen: *Actually, I think it might have something to do with when he was born, because he was premature and had to go in the special care baby unit. He was tiny and I remember being so scared that he wouldn't make it. I visited him twice a day when I was discharged from hospital. I remember feeling really numb. But he did OK and came home after a month. He was a happy baby and seemed to be doing fine until he went to nursery. He was so clingy. They had to peel him off me. He didn't settle and had temper tantrums, threw toys around and hit other children. It just got worse when he went up to reception class. He has a really nice teacher, who helps him calm down most of the time. I am worried that he might have to go to a special school and I just want him to be happy, behave himself and learn like all the other kids.*

Debi: *Thanks, Karen – that's really helpful for me to know. Sounds, really really tough. You're worried about what's going to happen to Daniel going forward.*

Karen: *I am very worried.*

Debi: *Can you tell me a bit about how Daniel feels about what's happening at school and home with his behaviour?*

Karen: *Well, he's happy when it's quiet. I think school's too loud and noisy for him sometimes. He likes his own space and to do things on his own terms. He's a bit stubborn, I guess. I worry that he hates school and doesn't want to go. I see him twiddling his hands in the car on the way and he makes me feel really anxious about dropping him off. Like something bad is going to happen.*

Appendix 8

Legend

Yellow	evidence of Karen's thoughts
Blue	evidence of Karen's own feelings
Purple	evidence that Karen recognises Daniel's thoughts
Pink	evidence that Karen recognises Daniel's feelings
Green	evidence that Karen understands that Daniel's behaviour makes her think and/or feel things
Grey	evidence that Karen understands that her behaviour makes Daniel think and/or feel things

Commentary

- Karen recognises some of her thinking and thoughts about Daniel
- Karen recognises some of her feelings about Daniel and his behaviour
- In this extract, there is no direct evidence of Karen recognising Daniel's own thoughts but there is some recognition of how he might be feeling
- There is one example of Karen recognising that Daniel's behaviour affects her thoughts and feelings
- In this extract, there is no evidence that Karen recognises that her own behaviour affects Daniel's thoughts and feelings

Appendix 9

Frequently asked questions

These are some of the questions that practitioners and parents/carers often ask.

Q: Can I deliver PCAP to both parents at the same time and how does the home playtime work?

A: Absolutely! Consider the needs of the child when planning the playtimes at home. It is still preferable for the child to have one playtime a week, so the parents alternate facilitating them. They can create one mini-kit between them or have "Dad" and "Mum" kits (or kits for both Dads, both Mums, Grandparents, as appropriate)

Q: Can I deliver PCAP to children under three?

A: The full PCAP method is sometimes fine. However, consider the developmental needs of the child. Asking a two-year-old to stay in the space could actually be punitive because she is only very small. However, the light version will work very well on any age, including very young children even babies.

Q: Can I add things to the playkit?

A: The mini-kit remains the same for the initial set of playtimes. After this it can be changed or replenished. The child may also have a few ideas of what to have in it.

Q: What if my child wants to add things to the playkit?

A: We simply say that this kit is what we have right now and is just for this playtime together.

Q: What if the child refuses to play during playtimes at home?

A: We let the child know that playtime is starting and we are ready and waiting if she wants to join us – it is up to her. The parent/carer remains ready for the agreed time and then packs up and lets the child know that we will play again next week. The parent/carer remains calm throughout. If the child arrives part of the way through, the parent/carer introduces the playtime as usual, but with the number of minutes remaining only. Again, the parent/carer is kind and calm throughout.

Q: Can parents/carers offer PCAP to their other children?

A: Absolutely – either the full or light method. It is probably a good idea to check that the parent/ carer is not taking on too much at once. One child at a time might be helpful!

Q: What if the child sabotages the playtimes and breaks all of the rules on purpose?

A: The "choices and consequences" approach is used just the same and the parent/carer remains calm throughout. In extreme cases, it may be better to move to using the one-step approach to ease this relationship.

References

Ainsworth, M. D. S., Blehar, M. C., Waters, E. and Wall, S. (1978) *Patterns of Attachment: A psychological study of the Strange Situation.* Hillsdale, NJ: Lawrence Erlbaum Associates.

Andreassen, C. and West, J. (2007) Measuring socio-economic functioning in a national birth cohort study. *Infant Mental Health Journal*, 28(6): 627–46.

Bammens, S., Adkins, T. and Badger, J. (2015) Psycho-educational intervention increases reflective functioning in foster and adoptive parents. *Adoption and Fostering*, 39(1): 38–50.

Baradon, T., Fonagy, P., Bland, K., Lenard, K. and Sleed, M. (2008) New Beginnings – an experience-based programme addressing the attachment relationship between mothers and their babies in prisons. *Journal of Child Psychotherapy*, 34(2): 240–58.

Baumrind, D. (1967). Child-care practices anteceding three patterns of preschool behavior. *Genetic Psychology Monographs*, 75, 43–88.

Beckwith, L., Cohen, S. E. and Hamilton, C. E. (1999) Maternal sensitivity during infancy and subsequent life events relate to attachment representation at early adulthood. *Developmental Psychology*, 35(3): 693–700.

Bowlby, J. (1969) *Attachment and loss I: Attachment.* New York: Basic Books.

Egeland, B. and Carlson, E. (2004) Attachment and psychopathology. In L. Atkinson and S. Goldberg (eds.) *Attachment issues in psychopathology and intervention.* Hillsdale, NJ: Lawrence Erlbaum Associates.

Fonagy, P. and Target, M. (1997) Attachment and reflective function: Their role in self-organization. *Development and Psychopathology*, 9(4): 679–700.

Fonagy, P., Gergely, G., Jurist, E. L. and Target, M. (2004) *Affect regulation, mentalization and the development of the self*. London: Karnac Books.

Fonagy, P., Steele, H., Moran, G., Steele, M. and Higgitt, A. (1991) The capacity for understanding mental states: The reflective self in parent and child and its significance for security of attachment. *Infant Mental Health Journal*, 12(3): 201–18.

Green, J. and Goldwyn, R. (2002) Annotation: Attachment disorganisation and psychopathology: New findings in attachment research and their potential implications for developmental psychopathology in childhood. *Journal of Child Psychology and Psychiatry*, 43(7): 835–46. doi: 10.1111/14697610.00102.

Greenberg, M. (1999) Attachment and psychopathology in childhood. In J. Cassidy and P. Shaver (eds.) *Handbook of attachment: Theory, research and clinical applications*. New York: Guilford Press.

Greenspan, S. (2006) Rethinking "Harmonious Parenting" using a three-factor discipline model. *Child Care in Practice*, 12(1): 5-12.

Grienenberger, J., Kelly, K. and Slade, A. (2005) Maternal reflective functioning, mother-infant affective communication, and infant attachment: Exploring the link between mental states and observed caregiving behavior in the intergenerational transmission of attachment. *Attachment and Human Development*, 7(3): 299–311.

Guerney, L. and Ryan, V. (2013) *Group Filial Therapy: The complete guide to teaching parents to play therapeutically with their children*. London: Jessica Kingsley Publishers.

Jones, T.L. and Prinz, R.J. (2005) Potential roles of parental self-efficacy in parent and child adjustment: A review. *Clinical Psychology Review*, 25, 341–63.

Kalland, M., Fagerlund, A., von Koskull, M. and Pajulo, M. (2016) Families First: The development of a new mentalization-based group intervention for first-time parents to promote child development and family health. *Primary Health Care Research and Development*, 17(1): 3–17.

Kearney, J. and Cushing, E. (2012) A multi-modal pilot intervention with violence-exposed mothers in a child treatment program. *Issues in Mental Health Nursing*, 33(8): 544–52.

Kendall S. and Bloomfield L. (2005) Developing and validating, a

References

tool to measure parenting self-efficacy. *Journal of Advanced Nursing*, 51(2): 174–81.

Lin, Y.-W. and Bratton, S. C. (2015) A meta-analytic review of child-centered play therapy approaches. *Journal of Counseling and Development*, 93(1): 45–58.

Maccoby, E. E., and Martin, J. A. (1983) Socialization in the context of the family: Parent–child interaction. In P. H. Mussen & E. M. Hetherington (eds.) *Handbook of child psychology: Vol. 4. Socialization, personality, and social development* (4th ed.). New York: Wiley.

Main, M. and Solomon, J. (1986) Discovery of a new, insecure disorganized/disoriented attachment pattern. In T. B. Brazelton and M. Yogman (eds.) *Affective development in infancy*. Norwood, New Jersey: Ablex.

Main, M. and Solomon, J. (1990) Procedures for identifying disorganized/disoriented infants during the Ainsworth Strange Situation. In M. Greenberg, D. Cicchetti and M. Cummings (eds.) *Attachment in the preschool years: Theory, research and intervention*. Chicago: University of Chicago Press.

Maskell-Graham, D. (2016) *Reflective functioning and play: Strengthening attachment relationships in families from pregnancy to adolescence*. Nottingham: big toes little toes.

Moutsiana, C., Fearon, P., Murray, L., Cooper, P., Goodyer, I., Johnstone, T. and Halligan, S. (2014) Making an effort to feel positive: Insecure attachment in infancy predicts the neural underpinnings of emotion regulation in adulthood. *Journal of Child Psychology and Psychiatry*, 55(9): 999–1008.

O'Connor, T. G. and Scott, S. B. C. (2007) *Parenting and outcomes for children*. York: Joseph Rountree Foundation.

Pajulo, M., Pyykkönen, N., Kalland, M., Sinkkonen, J., Helenius, H., Punamäki, R. and Suchman, N. (2012) Substance-abusing mothers in residential treatment with their babies: Importance of pre- and postnatal maternal Reflective Functioning. *Infant Mental Health Journal*, 33(1): 70–81.

Pajulo, M., Suchman, N., Kalland, M. and Mayes, L. (2006) Enhancing the effectiveness of residential treatment for substance abusing pregnant and parenting women: Focus on maternal reflective functioning and mother-child relationship. *Infant Mental Health Journal*, 27(5): 448–65.

Pawson, R. and Tilley, N. (1997) *Realistic evaluation*. London: SAGE.

Rispoli, K. M., McGoey, K. E., Kozid, N. A. and Schreiber, J. B. (2013) The relation of parenting, child temperament and attachment security in early childhood to social competence at school entry. *Journal of School Psychology*, 51(5): 643–58.

Schechter, D. S., Myers, M. M., Brunelli, S. A. and Coates, S. W. (2006) Traumatized mothers can change their minds about their toddlers: Understanding how a novel use of videofeedback supports positive change of maternal attributions. *Infant Mental Health Journal*, 27(5): 429–47.

Shai, D. (2010) Introducing Parental Embodied Mentalising: Exploring moments of meeting of mind of parent and infants from a relational whole-body kinaesthetic perspective. In S. Bender (ed.) *Movement analysis of interaction* (107–24). Berlin: Logos Verlag.

Shai, D. and Belsky, J. (2011) When words just won't do: Introducing Parental Embodied Mentalizing. *Child Development Perspectives*, 5(3): 173–80.

Slade, A. (2005) Parental Reflective Functioning: An introduction. *Attachment and Human Development*, 7(3): 269–82.

Slade, A. (2006) Reflective parenting programs: Theory and development. *Psychoanalytic Inquiry*, 26(4): 640–57.

Slade, A., Bernbach, E., Grienenberger, J., Levy, D. W. and Locker, A. (2005a) *The Pregnancy Interview. Manual for scoring*. New Haven, CT: Yale Child Study Center.

Slade, A., Grienenberger, J., Bernbach, E., Levy, D. and Locker, A. (2005b) Maternal reflective functioning, attachment, and the transmission gap: A preliminary study. *Attachment and Human Development*, 7(3): 283–98.

Sleed, M., Baradon, T. and Fonagy, P. (2013) New Beginnings for mother and babies in prison: A cluster randomised controlled trial. *Attachment and Human Development*, 15(4): 349–67.

Söderström, K. and Skårderud, F. (2009) Minding the Baby. Mentalisation-based treatment in families with parental substance use disorder: Theoretical framework. *Nordic Psychology*, 61(3): 47–65.

Stern, T. (2014) The development of Reflective Functioning in a mother traumatised by past and present events: Facilitating change in the parent-infant relationship. *Journal of Infant, Child, and Adolescent Psychotherapy*, 13(1): 24–36.

Suchman, N. E., DeCoste, C., Leigh, D. and Borelli, J. (2010) Reflective Functioning in mothers with drug use disorders: Implications for dyadic interactions with infants and toddlers. *Attachment and Human Development*, 12(6): 567–85.

Suess, G., Grossman, K. and Sroufe, A. (1992) Effects of infant attachment to mother and father on quality of adaptation in preschool: From dyadic to individual organisation of self. *International Journal of Behavioral Development*, 15(1): 43–65.

Tomlin, A., Strum, L. and Kock, S. (2009) Observe, listen, wonder, and respond: A preliminary exploration of reflective function skills in early care providers. *Infant Mental Health Journal*, 30(6): 634–47.

VanFleet, R. (2014) *Filial Therapy: Strengthening parent-child relationships through play (3rd ed.)*. Sarasota, FL: Professional Resource Press.

van Ijzendoorn, M. H., Schuengel, C. and Bakermans-Kranenburg, M. J. (1999) Disorganized attachment in early childhood: Meta-analysis of precursors, concomitants, and sequelae. *Development and Psychopathology*, 11(2): 225–49.

Weinfeld, N., Whaley, G., Egeland, B. and Carlson, E. (1999) The nature of individual differences in infant-caregiver attachment. In J. Cassidy and P. Shaver (eds.) *Handbook of attachment: Theory, research, and clinical applications*. New York: Guilford Press.

WHO (2004) *The importance of caregiver–child interactions for the survival and healthy development of young children: A review.* Department of Child and Adolescent Health and Development, World Health Organization.

Postscript from the author

Thank you very much for reading this book!

All proceeds from our books and online resources help fund our international outreach projects.

FREE PCAP RESOURCES FOR READERS!

Please visit our website for details of training, licensing and the free resources which accompany this book.

www.bigtoeslittletoes.org